ARMAMENT AND TECHNOLOGY

ANTI-TANK
WEAPONS
AND MILITARY VEHICLES

Illustrations: Octavio Díez Cámara, Acmat, AEROSPATIALE, Celsius Bofors Missiles, EUROMISSILE, IVECO Defense Vehicles Division, KBP, Lohr Industrie, Matra Bae Dynamics, Nissan Motor Ibérica, Patria Vehicles, Raytheon, Renault, Scania, Stewart & Stevenson, Tatra and Texas Instruments.

Production: Lema Publications, S.L.
Editorial Director: Josep M. Parramón Homs
Text: Octavio Díez
Editor: Eva Mª Durán
Coordination: Eduardo Hernández
Translation: Jennifer Murray
Original title: Medios contracarro y vehículos

© Lema Publications, S.L. 2000

ISBN 84-95323-30-3

Photocomposition and photomechanics: Novasis, S.A.L.
Barcelona (Spain)
Printed in Spain

ARMAMENT AND TECHNOLOGY

ANTI-TANK WEAPONS

AND MILITARY VEHICLES

LEMA
Publications

This second generation anti-tank missile is the result of the combined efforts of the German defense industry, Messerschimitt-Bölkow-Blohm GmbH, and the Division des Engins Tactiques of the French company, Aerospatiale, in the form of Euromissile (a company that has developed several advanced weapons systems such as the wire-guided anti-tank missile launcher MILAN).

Incorporated into the arsenals of more than forty countries, it has proven to be unparalleled in its effectiveness and simplicity. More importantly, it has demonstrated more uses in combat than previously believed. In addition, it can be deployed with great speed: in less than 50 seconds, the apparatus will separate from its means of transport (either a vehicle or helicopter), position itself, and consecutively fire two missiles at two targets located at average distances.

Designed to hold back the advance of armored formations

The political tensions between the West and the East after the end of World War II led military strategists to develop very powerful armies whose mission was to combat a hypothetical enemy invasion. With this philosophy in mind, the French and German governments signed an economic agreement to collaborate (thus reducing costs) on a new generation of anti-air and anti-tank

---

LAUNCH CONTAINER

The fiberglass tube located on the upper part of the stand, which serves as a means of support during the launch, contains in its interior the missile, a gas generator that is fired from the tube at a speed of 245 feet per second, and a thermal battery, which serves as the source of electricity.

COMPLETE VISION

A MIRA visual and thermal heat guiding device may be placed on the missile launcher, allowing for its unrestricted use in any weather conditions, particularly at night.

---

missiles, including several short and medium range systems. Thus, the two countries would guarantee their productive self-sufficiency and would be able to confront all types of air and land threats in a battlefield characterized by vast and mechanized armored formations.

The MILAN is born

The name "Missile Infanterie Léger ANtichar" —lightweight anti-tank infantry missile— was originally designed as a lightweight device to be integrated into the anti-tank defenses of small infantry formations. In 1963, research was begun to study the various missile and launcher alternatives with the goal of obtaining the highest degree of integration with the people that had to use them.

It wasn't until 1969 that a prototype was prepared and subjected to rigorous tests before deciding on its acquisition. The first shots from the definitive version were carried out during the course of 1972.

The following year, mass production was initiated, and the first models began to be distributed to the German Heer and the

The MILAN system has been installed in the back of a light off-road vehicle, a Nissan Patrol MC-4 belonging to the Spanish Paratrooper Brigade; it can be launched by parachute along with the troops.

French l'Armée de Terre. Great Britain joined the production group upon confirmation that this model (already developed and available) satisfied all their operational requirements.

Wide international distribution

The arrival of the Soviet tank T-72 caused a huge stir among NATO leaders who were informed that the device had a very advanced plate of armor that Western weapons systems could not penetrate. This information caused production on the MILAN to cease, and the German Defense Minister publicly announced his decision to cancel the contract. Yet this never happened since a new warhead was developed for the missile, giving rise to the MILAN 2 system, in service since 1984.

This minor incident did not, however, delay the sale of the missile to third world countries. At present, orders total almost 250,000 for missiles and 10,000 for launchers which, since 1996, has included the MILAN 3

ADVANCED DEVELOPMENT
The MILAN 3 includes various advances in comparison to past models. Among these is the elongated tube that projects forward and which makes it possible to explode the charge at the optimum distance from the armored tank to achieve the most damage.

with a more advanced missile that incorporates a warhead. It is intended to stand up to the most advanced armored tanks in such a way that clients with even the most antiquated systems can update their capacity simply by acquiring the new munitions. These systems are employed in their three configurations by 41 countries, including Saudi Arabia, Belgium, Egypt, Greece, Iraq, Iran, Morocco, Portugal,

Syria and Somalia. The production license has been ceded to Spain, Great Britain, India and Italy, countries that use the system in their armies.

EASY TO TRANSPORT
On the top of the firing mechanism there is a large, sturdy handle that allows for comfortable transport from vehicles or helicopters to the launch area.

Simple to use and transport

These two ideas characterize the design of this system, which has responded more than adequately to its users' needs. In addi-

tion, its lightness and speed combine with an excellent system of range, precision and destructive power. Considering the fact that it is designed for small infantry units and that it can be launched from positions on the ground or from all types of vehicles, it is multipurpose and has some significantly advanced operational criteria for the period in which it was devised. It has a maximum range of 6,570 feet, a very short minimum range that facilitates close combat with tanks, and reduced weight and dimensions which enable it to be moved; it is capable of being moved easily and quickly, even to unprepared positions. In addition, it completes its trajectory rapidly, has a firing frequency of at least 3 shots per minute, training on the easiest and least expensive methods of use, and a rate of reliability that exceeds 95%.

Overall presentation of the system

This anti-tank system is composed of four basic elements: the munitions, the firing mechanism, the controls and firing mechanism

GUARANTEED MOBILITY
A lightweight stand fixes the firing mechanism of the MILAN system to various types of vehicles including M-113 armored caterpillar tracks. In this way, the troops have the capacity to neutralize the threat of mechanized armored formations.

TECHNICAL CHARACTERISTICS OF THE MILAN 2 ANTI-TANK SYSTEM

COST OF THE MISSILE IN DOLLARS:	About 7,000	**Firing frequency**	3 or more shots per minute
DIMENSIONS AND WEIGHT:		**Head penetration**	40 inches in solid target at 0° angle;
Munitions length	47 in		115 mm penetrates heavy NATO tank target
Firing mechanism weight	37 lbs		at 65° angle
Missile weight	14.8 lbs	**Operating team**	Two men – a systems operator and reloading
PROPULSION:			assistant
Two-stage rocket engine with a combustion time of about 13 seconds.		**Launch pads**	May be assembled on the ground or in various
			vehicles including double turrets like the MCT
PERFORMANCE:		**Probability of impact**	Close to 100 % for immobile objects from 32 to
Range	From 80 to 4570 feet		40 inches at 2,630 feet distance, and 75 % for
Flying time	Up to 430 feet per second in the acceleration		objects at less than 985 feet
	phase which lasts 1.3 seconds, and up to 700 f/s		
	during the cruising phase which can last up to 11 s		

support, and the training simulator. The munitions include the missile with a two-stage rocket engine for the acceleration and cruising phases, a gyroscope, the thermal battery, the decoder, a daytime infrared tracer, the missile head with a charge of 4 pounds of explosives and an activation fuse. These are located within a fiberglass tube that serves as a container for all operations and as the launcher when it is fired.

The firing mechanism is used to aim at immobile and moving objects, and includes a compact automatic aiming and guiding device that is located on the firing stand on a small tripod on the lower part. The controls are used to confirm that it is functioning properly. Among them are a type S verification apparatus (in the form of a case that connects to the launcher for inspection), the equipment that verifies the correlation between the aiming axes and the missile launch, and testing equipment for the goniometer. The simulator, which is employed in association with the firing mechanism, reduces the number of real shots to a minimum and

EASY TO TRANSPORT

A metal harness allows for the placement of two full containers on the loader's shoulder as if it were a backpack, facilitating the transport of the missiles to the area where they will be used (photo at left).

SAFETY DURING FIRING

The smoke leaving the rear end of the fiberglass tube, which is used for the launching of the missile, forces the operator to leave a part of the back end free, so neither he nor his assistant are injured (photo at right).

considerably lowers the cost of operator training.

The various subsystems are normally transported in watertight containers, which allow them to be launched by paratroopers into the area of combat or transported in the interior of all types of vehicles, so that neither the firing mechanism nor the missiles suffer any damage. Some batches of missiles have been stored for almost twenty years

DURABLE AND SIMPLIFIED MECHANISM
This French and German system with its reduced size and weight of not much more than 35 pounds has the perfect combination of power and resistance to arm those infantry units that must travel extensively in the combat zone.

and, when finally used, have worked perfectly although they were not checked beforehand.

Guaranteed to work under any circumstances

The MILAN has a high operational level whether it is assembled on the ground or in a vehicle. It is easy to use and is normally operated by two men. One of them acts as the shooter and is in charge of transporting the launcher, and the other assists by carrying the two missile containers, ready to open fire immediately.

In order to work the firing mechanism, simply unfold the tripod and load the container. The lateral protective covers should have been previously removed so that both pieces fit together easily. The shooter normally lies on the ground to avoid the smoke and the stand and checks to see that the target is within range. Then he pushes the firing button, which activates the ignition sequence and successively sets in motion the battery supply, the electronic guide, the infrared goniometer, the missile gyroscope, the missile battery, the daytime and nighttime tracers and the gas generator. In 0.06 seconds, the tube shoots back about three meters, and the high-pressure gases produced by the generator eject the missile from the tube at a speed of 250 feet per second. The four fins automatically deploy, and the missile starts to fly about 20 inches above the line of aim toward the position designated by the operator, who only needs to keep the target centralized in the aiming scope, with a magnification of 7. The commands are automatically transmitted between the launcher and the missile, which are connected by a wire until impact. The piloting is done via a jet deflector that maneuvers on command. A thermal camera may be attached to the firing mechanism, which enables it to be used in complete darkness. It weighs 18.7 lbs and is attached via an adapter on the upper part of the viewfinder.

Operational experience in combat

The MILAN was deployed by the French and the British in the Persian Gulf against Iraq during Operation Desert Storm, by the Lebanese to slow down the movements of the Israeli armored forces, and by the Iraqis to destroy Iranian Chieftain tanks and helicopters. However, it proved especially effective during the war in the Falkland Islands. Thanks to the documentation available on this conflict, we know that the missiles were used by men in the 2nd Paratrooper Regiment, the 42nd Command of the Royal Marines and even by the Gurkhas. Shots were fired for at least two weeks at Argentinean defensive forces on Mount Harriet during the advance on Port Stanley, proving the system to be effective during the day as well as at night. In spite of the fact that a thermal camera was not available to neutralize medium and heavyweight machine guns, defensive posi-

AUTOMATIC GUIDE
The operator of the MILAN system must aim at a point of reference over the target, fire the missile and maintain the viewfinder centered on the target. Corrections are made automatically during the flight.

tions, command posts and equipment storage areas, this weapon, designed for anti-tank warfare, was used as a successful (but costly) means of artillery support for the infantry.

INTERIOR OF THE MILAN
This diagram shows the elements that make up the MILAN anti-tank missile and its container, which serves as a protective covering and facilitates the launch of the missile. Two important elements are the warhead, on the right side, and the propulsion, on the left.

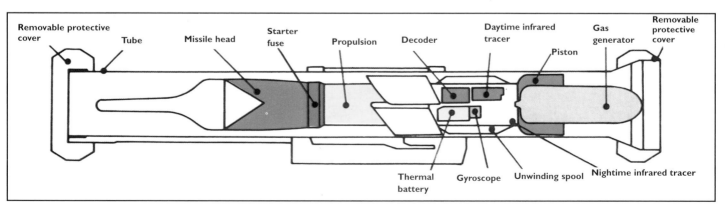

T he TOW anti-tank system is the most widely used medium-range option in the world. It has been chosen to equip ground launch pads and to arm helicopters in a multitude of countries.

To date, more than 40,000 models of this missile have been produced. Its notable performance, straightforward use, the possibility of buying it on credit at FMS (Foreign Military Sales), and the promising prospects of U.S. army support for buyers, if necessary, have caused its wide distribution. It must also be added that the system has continued evolving, receiving improvements in the missile and launch unit to adapt it to the new fighting potential of tanks.

Western development to neutralize Soviet tanks

The conception of this U.S. anti-tank system dates back to the 1970's. At that time, the U.S. army solicited proposals from various compa-

TRANSPORT DETAIL

The TOW anti-tank system may be used without difficulties in the back of the Hummer light vehicle. Six missile containers, the tripod, the launcher, the guide viewfinders, and the rest of the system's elements may be kept here.

nies for a system capable of facing Soviet tanks and destroying them from a distance far enough away that they could not respond by firing their 115 millimeter guns.

Transport detail
The TOW anti-tank system may be used

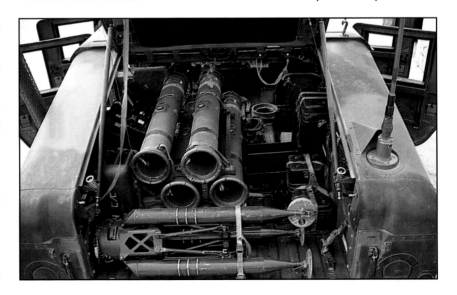

without difficulties in the back of the Hummer light vehicle. Six missile containers, the tripod, the launcher, the guide viewfinders, and the rest of the system's elements may be kept here.

The Hughes Aircraft company was chosen to develop the missile, and the design of a missile called BGM-71 TOW (Tube-launched, Optically-tracked, Wire-guided) was begun in 1962. The first test models were fired in 1968.

The system is tested in combat

Two years later, in the summer of 1972, it was used for the first time against North Vietnamese tank units. The missiles were assembled in frameworks called XM-26 —X for eXperimental— that had been installed in Bell UH-1B "Huey" helicopters. These systems gave good results against the PT-76 light tanks and medium T-54's; in one day, a single airplane destroyed six tanks and severely damaged a seventh one.

In 1973, thousands were sent to the Israelis to support them in the Yom Kippur War against the Egyptians, proving that the missile ground launchers were also very effective in this part of the world. As a result, they were used again (and again with optimal results) by the Israelis in 1982 against the Syrians in Operation Peace for Galilee which brought about the invasion of Lebanon in order to obtain a safety zone against terrorist attacks. Their helicopters de-

HEAVY EQUIPMENT

The TOW anti-tank system is heavy enough to require a light vehicle to transport it to the combat zone. It is usually fixed to a stand in the back of the vehicle and the missile containers are also anchored in specific places.

INSTALLED IN AN ARMORED VEHICLE

The TOW system may be fixed in its standard launching configuration or via more advanced turrets in various types of wheeled or chained armored vehicles. The BMR-TOW is one of those used by the Spanish "Brunete" division.

stroyed 29 tanks and 50 armored vehicles in a single day.

Second generation system

Its success in combat (including the first Gulf War between Iran and Iraq where it was widely used by the Iranians) brought about the development of an Improved model called ITOW, with an improved warhead and a connecting rod that could explode its charge on the ground at an ideal distance. Then the TOW 2 was produced, a variation which incorporates a bigger explosive head, an improved digital guiding system and a new rocket engine.

Between 1988 and 1991, work was carried out on an alternate system now known as the BGM-71F TOW 2B. 2,406 units of this missile were produced at once and charged to the 1990 U.S. budget; afterwards, several batches of 10,000 units were manufactured annually. Among the improvements is a head with two blank charges that face downward.

Easy to use

To use this wire-guided system, the operator fixes the reticle of the aiming device on the target to be destroyed. While keeping the object centralized, he pulls the trigger that activates the firing process and ignites the rocket engine of the missile, which then begins to fly at the target at a speed of almost Mach 1.

The missile starts to advance toward the target as the infrared source at the rear is

located by the search equipment of the guiding system. In this way, the signal detected is sent to the guiding mechanism, which determines the flight pattern and transmits to the missile (via the double wire that joins them) the necessary commands for it to move its fins so that it is aiming at the target. This automatic operation allows for any corrections necessary throughout the twenty second flight. Therefore, the projectile is guaranteed to follow the signaled trajectory in order to reach the point of impact, which may be fixed or in motion.

An effective model with an excellent reputation

The availability and effectiveness of this system —which should preferably be used on an air or ground launch pad since its considerable weight limits its transportation— is excellent. In addition, operators may be trained in its use in a short period of time with the help of a specific training system. This, along with the fact that countries that are "friends" of the U.S. may easily purchase them, has been a determining factor for the

DEPLOYED BY THE MARINES

The anti-tank units of the U.S. Marine Corps trust the TOW anti-tank missile system to neutralize the armor-plated threats that may be encountered on the beachhead or during their advances into the interior of the battle.

large number of nations who possess the missile. Among these countries are Germany, Saudi Arabia, Bahrain, Canada, South Korea, Denmark, Egypt, Spain, Finland, Greece, Italy, Japan, Jordan, Kuwait, Luxembourg, Morocco, Portugal, Thailand and Turkey.

Launching platforms adapted to every necessity
In addition to its ground launch pad, which

COMPLETE MOBILITY

The installation of the TOW system in light off-road vehicles provides ample room in which it can fire its missiles and quickly change positions so as not to be hit by enemy fire.

includes a tripod so that it may used from protected positions on any type of terrain, the TOW is easily transported by several methods. Off-road vehicles that may be installed with lightweight stands include the M151, the Hummer or the Spanish Patrols. In armored vehicles, the M901 ITV system is made up of a double turret located on an M-113, which is modified so that its operation and reloading are carried out by the crew from the inside. Other armored systems include the German Wiesel TOW, the U.S. Marines' Piranha 8x8 LAW, the M2/M3 "Bradley" with a double launcher attached to the main turret, and the Italian Dardo HIFIST with two launchers situated on the sides of the turret of this caterpillar track combat vehicle. The first 200 units of this last model have already been ordered.

Helicopters, ranging from the small Hughes 500 MD to the heavy AH-64 "Apache", tend to employ all kinds of lightweight platforms. Others include the Italian Augusta A109, the British Westland Lynx, the German MBB BO-105, and the U.S. AH-1 "Cobra", Sikorsky S-76M, and Bell 206-L-3 "Texas Ranger". Some of them can transport up to eight missiles ready to be used against all types of ground targets from more than 2.5 miles away. This lengthens the maximum range of the missile because it takes advantage of the inertia of the aircraft at the moment of launching.

DAY AND NIGHT CAPACITY
The TOW-LWL system has been brought up to date by the Spanish company INDRA and includes a very advanced guiding system, which allows it to be fired during the day or at night and can detect enemy movements within a radius of close to 4.5 miles.

EASY TO RELOAD
The missiles come inside protective containers that are used to launch them toward the target. One man can reload the container rapidly and easily.

Lightweight variant developed in Spain

An agreement between the U.S. company Raytheon Systems and the Spanish Empresa Nacional de Óptica (ENOSA) of the INDRA group which was signed at the end of 1992, and supported by the purchase of 200 launchers and 2,000 missiles by the Spanish army for a price of more than 11,000 million Spanish pesetas, brought about the development of the LWL (LightWeight Launcher). The initial weight was reduced by 25% and the number of parts was also lowered from 11 to 5. An automatic system verifies the state of its components, and a new, unique guiding system with a thermal camera supplied with a second generation IR HgCdTe sensor was also installed. Operating within a frequency of 8 to 12 nanometers, the sensor has proven capable of locating an object 7.5 miles away and projecting its image with remarkable resolution on a CRT screen. Thus, the operator can verify the location of the enemy without being noticed.

MISSILE CONTAINER

A fiberglass tube, which can be easily transported by one man, constitutes the tactical packaging of the missile. It is also used to aim the weapon at the objective.

REAR SURVEILLANCE

One of the three system operators stands so that he can see the rear, and use his rifle if necessary. This way, no enemy threat can surprise the rearguard.

FIRING OUTLET

When it is ignited, the missile is fired from the front part of the launcher toward the target. If possible, it is recharged as soon as it has completed its flight.

SUPPLY BOX

This auxiliary element provides the system with electricity previous to the launch. It contains the connection parts and the controls necessary for the operation.

STURDY LAUNCHER

The TOW system launcher has a sturdy, but lightweight articulated tripod. The photo above illustrates the central part where the three legs are joined to the main element, which supports the launcher and the guiding apparatus.

GUIDING SYSTEM

The U.S TOW-2B systems include a double-module missile guiding unit. The lower one corresponds to the two daytime viewing channels, and the upper one to the nightsight, which is used for observation as well as guiding the missile.

AIMING PASSAGE

On the upper part of the tripod there is a plated element which houses the missile launching containers. It is also used to regulate the direction and elevation, which enables the launchers to aim at the target.

SHOOTER

Three men are normally needed to operate this long-range U.S. anti-tank system, but only one maneuvers the guiding and tracking systems that permit the launch of the missile.

TECHNICAL CHARACTERISTICS OF THE TOW 2 ANTI-TANK SYSTEM

COST OF THE MISSILE IN DOLLARS:	20, 000
DIMENSIONS:	
Length before launch	47.28 in
Length after launch	67.53 in
Diameter	5.79 in
WEIGHT:	
Launcher	205 lbs
Missile container	61.9 lbs
Missile	47.4 lbs
Explosive charge	blank charge of 13 lbs
PROPULSION:	
Two-phase rocket engine with solid propellant	

PERFORMANCE:	
Range	From 200 to 12,300 feet if launched from the ground and more than 13,000 from helicopters
Speed	Mach 1
Flying time	21 seconds
Penetration	More than 800 mm into homogeneous armor
Shelf life of missile in container	More than 10 years

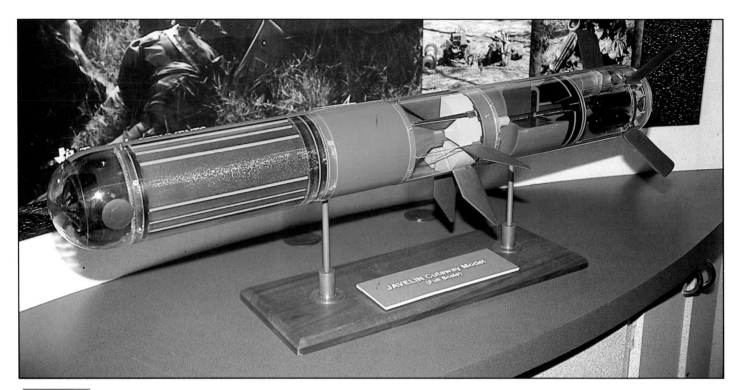

The technological and industrial advances gradually being made in different products in the defense industry have resulted in a higher level of performance for weapons and weapons systems.

A range of third generation portable anti-tank missiles are being produced, and a fourth is now being developed with a much more advanced guiding system and penetration capability. These advances allow for the development of systems that are more lightweight, capable and economical and are usually purchased by armies with generous funds. A good example of this are the most recent productions of the French Eryx system, the U.S. Javelin, and the Swedish BILL 2, which vary from short to medium range.

CONFIGURATION OF THE JAVELIN

This view of the Javelin anti-tank missile system shows its interior. Observe, from front to back, the automatic guiding apparatus, the explosive charge, the rocket engine, and the various flight mechanisms.

ZENITHAL ATTACK

The missiles of the BILL 2 anti-tank system have the capacity to attack the most vulnerable area of combat tanks, normally the upper part of the main turret. They detonate their explosive charge, capable of neutralizing present dangers, on the turret thanks to a close range fuse.

French mini-missile to arm the infantries

The French company Aerospatiale initiated the design of a very lightweight missile in the mid-1980's with the goal of producing a weapon that would increase the operational possibilities of the various types of rocket launchers being incorporated into the armies of several countries. This system was intended to be economical enough so that its price would not hinder its sale among possible buyers. In theory, the Eryx missile was to cost one-seventh the price of the MILAN missile and one-third of its launcher. The first order came from the French army, which wished to purchase 2,500 launchers and 50,000 pounds of ammunition to equip all its troops, replacing the ACL-89 STRIM rocket launchers with the APILAS. Subsequently, the first requests for exportation began arriving, leading to its sale in countries such as Brazil, Canada,

Malaysia and Norway. All in all, the orders total about 25,000 missiles.

Lightweight and effective

For its design and performance features, the Eryx is considered to be a short-range weapon capable of reaching targets between 164 and 1970 feet away. It can be used from the operator's shoulder or lying down, and it is very easy to prepare to fire. It can even be operated inside of confined spaces where its low level of smoke is essential. Only one man is required to transport and fire the system. It may also be employed at night thanks to the Mirabel thermal camera attached. It also includes a warhead capable of penetrating the most modern tanks and destroying blockades and bunkers.

This weapon uses a conventional and re-usable SACLOS wire-guided system that allows the shooter to control the movements of the missile thanks to a thrust control atta-ched to its nozzles. Thus, he can localize and follow the target via an optical viewfinder, with a magnification of three and a field of vision of 200 milliradians, which includes a CCD sensor to detect the position of the source of the infrared rays (IR) situated at the

BILL LAUNCHER
The launcher of the Swedish BILL system has a collapsible tripod, which compensates for irregulari-ties in the terrain, a guiding appara-tus attached to the left side, and a container that holds the missile prior to the launch.

FRENCH MISSILE
The photograph shows the shapes and internal distribution of the various components that make up the French Eryx missile, known for its powerful penetration capability in spite of its reduced size.

rear end of the missile. The guiding com-mands are generated by a tiny processor, with VLSI circuits, capable of resisting electronic counter measures.

With a flying time of 3.6 seconds required to reach its maximum range, the Eryx has a launcher that weighs 7.5 lbs and munitions that weigh 24.2 lbs. The explosive charge is

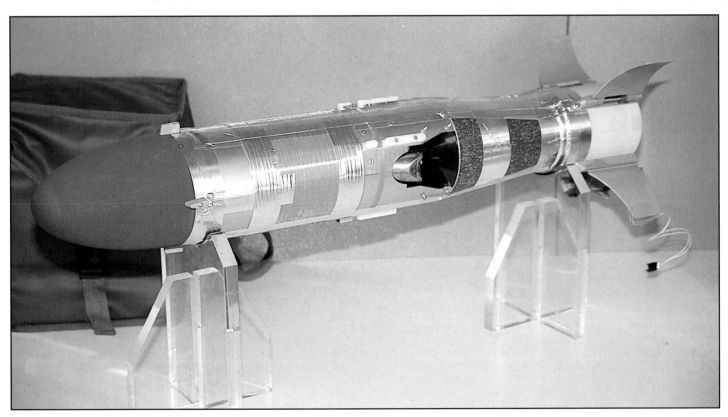

TECHNICAL CHARACTERISTICS OF THE JAVELIN ANTI-TANK SYSTEM

COST OF THE MISSILE IN DOLLARS:	26,000		PERFORMANCE:	
DIMENSIONS:			Range	656 feet
Length	42.6 in		Time needed to fire	30 seconds
Diameter	5 in		Time needed to reload	20 seconds
WEIGHT:			Shelf life in container	10 years
Guiding unit	14.11 lbs		Type and life of battery	BA lithium that lasts four hours
Container	9.04 lbs		**OPERATING TEAM:**	Two men
Missile	26 lbs		**LAUNCH PADS:**	Portable on the shooter's shoulder
PROPULSION:			**PROBABILITY OF IMPACT:**	95 %
Two-phase rocket engine with solid propellant				

blank, weighs 7.9 lbs and can penetrate more than 900 millimeters into homogenous armor. In addition, the missiles are driven by a small rocket engine (80 grams of solid propellant) that launches them from the container at a speed of 100 feet per second. It also incorporates a main engine that can reach a speed of 900 f/s and is mounted on the front of the weapon. The missile wich was a diameter of 4.3 inches and a length of 36.4 inches deploys, on leaving the container, four fins. These mesure that the missile maintains the connect flight path to the target.

U.S. system of "fire and forget"

The need to replace the M47 DRAGON system and the tactical possibilities associated with the new technologies led the U.S to work on a very advanced anti-tank missile system, whose range is 1.3 miles and may be used without restrictions from confined spaces or protected positions. The work was a result of the combined efforts of Lockheed Martin and Texas Instruments.

The EMD program (Engineering, Manufacturing and Development) for development and production was carried out quickly and consisted of more than 200 test shots. After confirming its advanced level of performance —which has proven lethal against the most advanced combat tanks and has ample operational possibilities against multiple threats— distribution of the system among the U.S. army troops stationed at Fort Benjamin was begun in June 1996. The marines are expected to receive their first missiles during 1999.

EASY TO MANEUVER
Aiming the Eryx is simple because the gunner need only maintain the target centralized in the reticle for a maximum of 3.6 seconds, which is the flight length for the missile's maximum range of 1,970 feet. It can be fired without restrictions from confined spaces thanks to its low level of firing smoke.

Integration of the most advanced and capable guiding system

Modular technology applied to the construction of this system has significantly reduced the cost while, at the same time, granting it the power to combat any possible enemy threats into the second decade of the next century. This is possible because its design is based on the CLU (Command Launch Unit), which may be employed to observe enemy forces during the day or at night, thanks to the integration of a passive thermal channel called FLIR (Forward Looking Infra-Red) attached to the disposable fiberglass tube that holds the missiles.

Using the missile is very straightforward; the operator only has to center the target in his viewfinder, fix on it with an activator and fire. The missile guides itself automatically toward the objective without any connection wires or further commands. In this way, the

missile operator and the person waiting to reload can quickly change positions to combat other targets or avoid enemy fire.

It is very easy to use thanks to the effectiveness of the associated training systems, which include basic (BST) and tactical equipment (FTT). Among its features, two interesting elements are the fact that the CLU weighs 14 lbs and its lithium battery has a life of four hours. Each missile weighs 26 lbs and measures 42.63 inches in length. There is a double warhead, and the rocket motor uses a solid propellant. Reloading takes 20 seconds, and the preparation time before firing is 30 seconds.

OPERATIONAL OPTIONS

The BILL, a medium-range anti-tank missile system, incorporates the possibility of choosing between four different attack modes according to the type of impact desired –direct or zenithal.

NOCTURNAL CAPACITY OF THE ERYX

The Eryx, a short-range anti-tank system, comes with a very compact Mirabel thermal camera. This may be used at night without restrictions against targets located within a radius of 1,970 feet.

The Swedish industry updates their production capacity

The BILL system, produced by Bofors Missiles of the Celsius group, whose headquarters is in Karlskoga, was created at the request of the Swedish army in 1979 and was introduced several years later and officially designated as RBS 56. In order to be the first to develop a more advanced system, they decided to incorporate several technological improvements such as the installation of a laser diode on the rear end of the missile that emits a previously established frequency. Therefore, the exact position can be determined, and there is no need to discriminate, as is the case with those systems that use an infrared source, between other possible emissions from the battlefield. An advanced warhead with a blank charge pointing downwards was also designed so that it could be used to neutralize the upper section of combat tanks —which are normally the least protected areas— as long as they are within the 7,225 that encompass its maximum range.

System configuration

The configuration of this system includes the missile and firing unit. The first —which incorporates a rocket engine with enough combustible for 2.2 seconds or a flight length

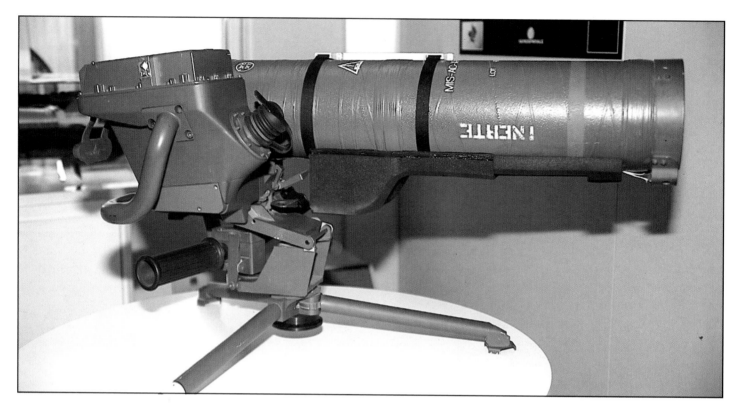

of 12 seconds— is already produced in the variant BILL 2 that also has a double explosive head in a vertical position. Thus, the explosion of the first missile activates the detonation of the reagent armor on some tanks or debilitates the multi-layered shield, and the second missile penetrates the main plate of armor.

This specific capacity can be selected before launching from four firing modules: the anti-tank (which activates the sensors and fires the missile along the line of fire), the anti-armor (which includes a special algorithm to combat these type of threats), a module against secondary targets (in which the missile flight corresponds to the line of fire but resorts to a direct impact fuse), and another against secondary targets (in which the optical sensor provokes a delayed detonation).

The firing unit includes a tripod which can be adjusted for height —to compensate for irregularities in the terrain— and a guiding system installed in an aluminum box attached to its exterior. This contains the aiming scope, the positioning unit of the missile and the electronics that process the signals from the guiding unit. These signals generally follow the OTA mode (Over-fly Top Attack),

LIGHTWEIGHT AND FUNCTIONAL

The features of the French system, Eryx, make it an ideal substitute for long-range anti-tank rocket launchers with regard to performance, capacity and price.

which means the missile flies 40 inches above the line of aim in order to hit its targets in their most vulnerable section.

LIGHTWEIGHT UNIT

The guiding unit of the Javelin is very compact and easy to transport. Its weight of only 14 lbs allows it to be used even among those troops that must travel extensively over all types of terrain.

The use of reagent armor in the new generation of Soviet combat tanks forced NATO members to question their ability to effectively neutralize them. This led to the initiation of various multinational projects to develop new systems capable of battling them. These projects included new munitions for the tanks, armed with smart guiding units launched by mortar or aircraft, and a third generation of more capable and more powerful anti-tank missiles.

Multinational project to cut costs

The price of researching and developing a new weapons system and the high cost of producing the thousands of units necessary to replace more antiquated systems led some members of NATO to sign a multinational protocol.

Under the leadership of the company EUROMISSILE Dynamics Group (EMDG), formed in 1979 by France, Great Britain and the now defunct Federal Republic of Germany, an agreement was reached to jointly develop a third generation weapon with the designations PARS-3, ATGW 3 or AC3G.

These countries were joined by Belgium, Spain, Greece, Holland and Italy, who were all very eager to participate in work on the new missile.

Variants of the weapon are produced to fulfill various requirements

In 1983, a schedule was established to outline the phases of development of two types of missiles: a medium-range one to replace the MILAN, and a long-range one that would substitute the HOT and TOW; each variant was to use the same components as the model it was replacing.

The first, designated as TRIGAT-MR (Medium Range), used the same configuration

as the MILAN. The launcher and guiding system are located on a small tripod so that the operator must bend down to aim, thus keeping his appearance to the enemy to a minimum. The missile, designed to arm the infantry, must incorporate a motor with a low level of initial firing smoke in order to be used in urban combat and in the interior of buildings. The guiding system, superimposed by a laser beam, is invulnerable to counter measures and eliminates any problems associated with the wire-guide in combat.

The TRIGAT-LR (Long-Range) was born out of the need for a system capable of facing any possible enemy threats predicted for the early decades of the 21st century. This involved a system that could be installed on helicopters or ground launch pads, was self-operating after being launched, and incorporated an explosive charge with two blank charges pointing forwards.

The companies divide up the work on the project

Representatives of the three countries heading up the development of the new model began the distribution of responsibilities from a joint planning office in Paris. The EMDG subcontracted the French company, Aerospatiale, the German, Messerschmitt-Bölkow-Blohm (MBB), and English, British Aerospace.

Aerospatiale was assigned to work on the optical electronics of the aiming and detection devices and also had the responsibility for the MR variant. MBB was in charge of the warhead

PREPARED FOR DEPLOYMENT

After a long process of research and development lasting more than twenty years, mass production was begun in 1999 on this third generation European anti-tank system with a superior capacity and level of performance.

GUIDING UNIT

The daytime guiding unit is located on the launcher's lower left side. The thermal camera, which allows for its use at night, is attached to it.

in collaboration with Royal Ordenance and SERAT, and British Aerospace took charge of the passive guiding unit of the LR version. Belgium, Spain and Italy also participated in the work. These last two countries withdrew from the project soon afterwards, claiming their depleted economies could not support such an outlay. They subsequently decided to head up their own projects which, in Spain's case, led to the acquisition of the U.S. TOW system and the modernization of its guiding unit and lightweight tripod by the defense industry.

The work continued along at a good pace, although various crises took place that threatened to cancel the project. In 1996, technical and military evaluation of the MR version was begun and included test sites as far away as Australia; mass production is predicted to begin in the year 2000.

A gestation that has lasted two decades

From 1978, when the feasibility phase was begun, to 1999, when production was finally started on the MR variant (and two more years for the LR), it has taken more than twenty years to design, develop, and evaluate a new family of missiles that will be the point of reference against which all other models in the next two decades will be measured. However, it remains to be seen what improved variants, designed with the current models in mind, can continue to be used in the next fifteen years.

The medium-range TRIGAT, very easy to transport and use

In 1997, Great Britain, claming that costs had shot up due to the large number of companies participating in one form or another in developing the different parts, demanded a reduction in the price by 15 %, or else they would abandon the project just before production was to begin. This problem forced the parties to sign a new agreement.

Apart from these inconvenient beginnings, the MR version of the TRIGAT is a very powerful option that incorporates the most advanced technology. Among the most interesting details is the guiding system made up of a low-energy laser beam emitted from the firing mechanism and followed by the missile. This is possible thanks to a receptor located at the rear. It is a method that is difficult to interfere with, since the emission is coded, and it makes it possible to change targets after the launch.

It can be used during the day and at night because of its third generation infrared sensor called an IRCCD (InfraRed Charge Coupled Device), which is available in two versions. The difference between them is that one is stored in a bottle of compressed air and the other

MISSILE CONFIGURATION

This container, which holds a TRIGAT-MR missile, shows the distribution and location of the interior elements. In particular, notice the red-colored blank charge in tandem in the center.

uses a closed-cycle cold compressor. It can hit fixed or moving targets. It incorporates a main engine with three nozzles that push on the center of gravity to give it exceptional maneuverability, even against objectives moving at speeds of 90 mph.

The system is basically composed of a launch stand and the containers that hold the munitions. The first incorporates a self-testing system that checks the guiding unit and thermal camera for any malfunctions. In

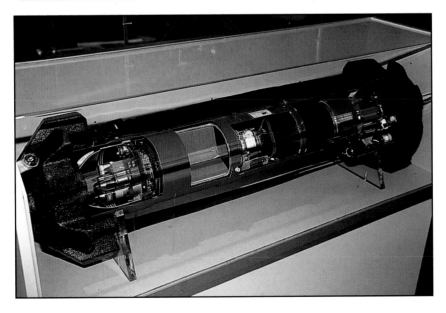

TECHNICAL CHARACTERISTICS OF THE TRIGAT-MR ANTI-TANK SYSTEM

COST IN DOLLARS:	Undecided		PERFORMANCE:	
RANGE:			Range	From 655 to 7880 feet
Length	41.17 in		Speed	
Diameter	152 mm		Flying time	Less than 12 seconds at 6,565 feet
WEIGHT:			Temperature of use	-50° F – 160° F
Firing mechanism	37.5 lbs		Penetration	
Missile container	37.5 lbs		**OPERATING TEAM:**	System operator and man to transport containers
Missile	33 lbs			
Thermal camera	from 15 to 20.64 lbs according to coolant		**LAUNCH PADS:**	From ground or attached to all types of vehicles
PROPULSION:				
Acceleration engines for the initial launch phase and engine with three nozzles for flight toward target			**PROBABILITY OF IMPACT:**	In excess of 90 %

addition, it is capable of a rapid firing pace, over 3 shots per minute. The munitions have a multi-purpose warhead with a blank charge in tandem, tiny acceleration motors which produce a speed of only 65 f/s during the launch, and may be used in closed spaces without injuring the operators with the initial smoke. The projectiles require no maintenance once they are stored in the launch containers. They are immune to shots fired from light-weight arms and enemy interference, resist nuclear, biological and chemical aggressions (NBQ), and can be reloaded in less than five seconds.

The long-range TRIGAT will equip the Tiger helicopter

The LR version of this European missile is much larger than its predecessor and has been equipped with new fins that give it the necessary stability to accurately hit its assign-

LONG-RANGE CAPACITY
The TRIGAT-LR was designed to hit targets located 3 miles away, but there is also a variant of increasing range that can neutralize tanks and other armored vehicles within a radius of 5 miles.

ed target. Development and tests have been significantly delayed because it is mainly intended to arm the French/German attack helicopter, Tiger, whose production is being held up for economic motives, among other things. Nevertheless, research is also being carried out on ground versions that would include launch turrets in medium vehicles.

The missile has a range of between 1,640 and 16,420 feet, which may be increased up to 26,265 feet at the client's request. This means the launch pad cannot be hit easily by the anti-air defenses of the enemy. The air variant includes a guiding system which a OSIRIS rotating/stabilizing viewfinder which is mounted on a pole over the rotor, an ATA firing command system, and two containers with four missiles in each that can fire off a round of four in only eight seconds. The guiding system is completely self-operating of the type "fire and forget", as the missile head

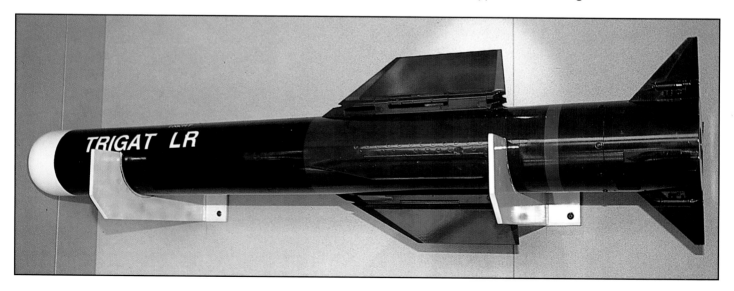

TRIGAT LR

incorporates a system that fixes on the target. The ground variant will be very similar in terms of conception, usage and results. The double blank charge in tandem warhead incorporates the possibility of selecting, before the launch, between a direct attack against targets, such as boats, helicopters, bridges or casemates, or hitting the upper section of armored tanks and vehicles. At the moment, the research continues. The system was mounted in a Tiger prototype at the beginning of 1996, and the first shot was fired March 12, 1998. Production is predicted to begin in 2001 after the system has gone through all the operational tests that will ensure it performs as expected.

TACTICAL DEPLOYMENT

The tubes with TRIGAT missiles are transported in special containers that protect them from damage. Two of them may be air launched with the tactical packaging shown in the photo.

THIRD GENERATION

In this photo, observe the container that can hold four long-range missiles (TRIGAT-LR) on the wing of this Tiger attack helicopter. They can be used to neutralize the armored formations of the enemy from a secure position.

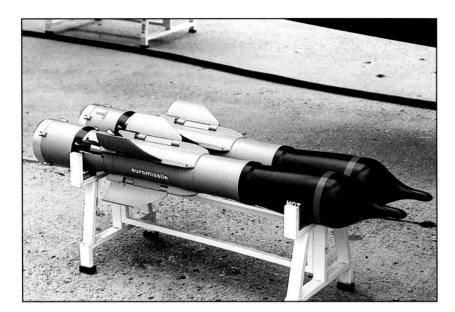

I n order to support the movements of an army's own armored formations and block the enemy's advance, it is necessary to use powerful methods with great destructive potential. One of these methods is the French-German HOT, designed as a long-range anti-tank weapon with superior penetration capabilities. The missile has proven very effective in these areas since it was entered into service at the beginning of the 1970's.

Since that time, it has become the principal long-range system of various European and Middle Eastern countries. Its variants have been installed in all types of land vehicles and on the sides of helicopters that are searching out tanks or working on reconnaissance missions.

Joint development to satisfy common requirements

The politics of military rapprochement between France and Germany during De Gaulle's term in office fostered relations between the industries in both countries to collaborate on the development of various weapons systems. Some, like anti-air and anti-tank missiles, were successful, while others failed, such as the design for a combat tank that would have been the first European model and the basis of later projects.

Subsonic missile guided by an optical system

In 1963, as the result of the collaboration

> **DESIGN FEATURES**
>
> The HOT 2 is a second generation anti-tank missile with a classic configuration: the explosive charge is colored black and is located at the front; the engine goes from the center until the back end of the fins (which stabilize the missile during flight), and the guiding unit is at the rear.

between the two countries' respective armies, a project was undertaken to design a very powerful and capable weapon, which the French called HOT (Haut subsonique Optiquement Teleguide).

This name was to refer to a second generation long-range anti-tank missile designed to replace the older systems in service at that time, such as the SS.11, which was improved in terms of general performance and penetration capability. Production was assigned to EUROMISSILE, made up of the German company, Messerschmitt-Bölkow-Blohm GmbH (MBB), and the French Aérospatiale. Work was begun in 1966, and the first prototype was tested in 1971 from a modified AMX-13 tank and an Alouette III helicopter.

During the tests, an average of 98 % of the targets were hit, and a rapid process of production was soon begun; the missiles and launchers were ready for operational testing by the French and German armies only two years later.

Mass production was begun in 1977; the missiles were distributed to the troops in 1978, and by the mid-1980's, more than 100,000 units had been ordered and delivered

TECHNICAL CHARACTERISTICS OF THE HOT 2 ANTI-TANK MISSILE

COST IN DOLLARS:	Unknown, although it varies from client to client
DIMENSIONS:	
Length	51.2 in
Exterior diameter	6.895 in
WEIGHT:	
Missile container	70.5 lbs
Missile	51.8 lbs
Explosive charge	14.3 lbs
	(9 lbs are explosives)
PROPULSION:	
Accelerating engine with four nozzles and cruising rocket engine with solid combustible	

PERFORMANCE:	
Range	13,100 feet launched from ground, and 14,100 from aircraft
Speed	785 f/s
Flying time	17.1 seconds
Conditions of use	-40° F – +126° F
Penetration	Between 31.5 and 47.2 into homogeneous armor
PROBABILITY OF IMPACT:	In excess of 90 %

to countries like Saudi Arabia, Egypt, Spain, Iraq, Libya, Syria and Kuwait. Production was subsequently undertaken on the HOT 2, which included a bigger and more powerful explosive head capable of penetration up to 47 inches. The HOT 3 has been available since 1997; it incorporates a double warhead and a close-range laser fuse. These features have caused it to be sold in a total of 18 countries.

The most varieties of launch pads
The flexibility of this system has allowed for

the development of various launch stands, among them air and ground launch pads. The ground pads range from single tube launchers (some of them French models) installed in Peugeot P4 light off-road vehicles to sophisticated systems with automatic reloading like the K3S, used by the Germans.

Among the most interesting models is the HCT turret, a lightweight installation with reduced dimensions and a weight of 92.6 pounds, which is made up of a stand with a viewfinder in the center and two launch tubes at the sides. The Lancelot system, intended for installation on armored caterpillar tracks, has a laser rangefinder and various optics that increase its weight to 2,910 lbs. The K3S is a hydraulic missile launcher with a supply of 8 munitions designed to be installed on the German Jagdpanter caterpillar fighter-tanks; the tanks are modified so that the launch module is situated behind the driver, and the shooter maneuvers the guide periscope located in the center of the vehicle at the front.

Various systems have been created to arm helicopters including a lightweight one with a SFIN rotating stabilizer viewfinder at the top of the apparatus, above the shooter, and two triple stands installed on the sides to hold the missile containers. This configuration is used by the Spanish and German BO-105 helicopters. The systems of the French Gazelle and those designed for the Dauphin are even more effective. The first is composed of two double launchers and a Viviane viewfinder,

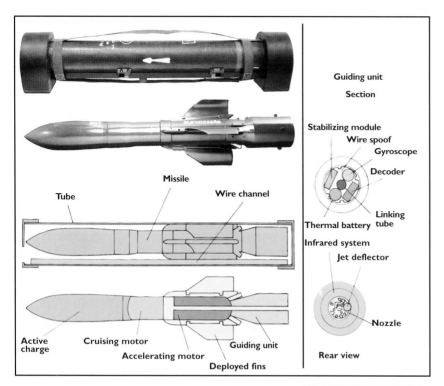

Tube

Missile

Wire channel

Guiding unit
Section

Stabilizing module
Wire spoof
Gyroscope
Decoder
Thermal battery
Linking tube
Infrared system
Jet deflector

Active charge

Cruising motor

Accelerating motor

Guiding unit

Deployed fins

Nozzle

Rear view

which incorporates the optical guiding unit, a laser rangefinder to determine the exact location of the target, and a thermal camera that can be operated in any weather conditions. In contrast, the second combines the Viviane with two quadruple missile contain-

INTERNAL CONFIGURATION

This diagram shows, among other things, the placement of the various components of the tube container and missile, and the location of the electronic elements in the guiding system.

ers. These containers, carrying HOT 3 missiles, can be used by the Tiger attack helicopters until the Trigat-LR missiles are ready, sometime in the middle of the next decade.

Powerful enough to damage the most protected tanks

The operational criteria of the HOT specify a longer range than the cannons of tanks so that it can attack from secure positions of up to 14,100 feet away, if fired from an aircraft. It has a high level of precision independent of its distance from the target, a maximum flying time of 17.3 seconds, and a high level of cooperation between active and launched mass so that it can penetrate armored vehicles with a capability not previously predicted for several decades.

The design criteria show its effectiveness

The qualities of this weapon, in particular its flexibility, have helped bring about its enormous success (especially taking into account that it must compete with the U.S. TOW), and stimulated its export to other countries. At the same time, it has allowed for

SUPERIOR RESPONSE CAPACITY

The semiautomatic launchers that can be installed in wheeled or chained armored vehicles vary according to what is needed. However, all of them incorporate a missile guiding unit, and the missile containers are ready to be fired.

TANK DESTROYER

The UTM 800 system is a turret that may be installed in armored vehicles, like this Panhard M3 VTH, and includes a guiding system with a APX M 509 viewfinder and four missiles ready to be fired. It weighs about 1,984 pounds and is reloaded manually.

so that the missile stays on track; these commands are transmitted by a wire that joins the launch stand to the missile.

In order to operate the guiding system, it has been designed in accord with some of the elements that constitute the munitions, the guiding equipment, and the launch and munitions stands. These systems can adopt various positions according to the launch pad and performance that is required.

Containers that can be stored with almost no further upkeep

The munitions are composed of a missile that comes packaged inside a fiberglass launch tube, which is used for transportation and storage. It is also used as the launch unit by pointing it toward the point of desired impact and attaching to the ends two protective covers, joined by a strap, that serve as tactical packaging.

This missile has an acceleration engine that can accelerate to a speed of 785 f/s in one second and maintain this speed throughout the flight thanks to a cruising engine of solid propellant produced by SNPE. It also has a blank active charge attached to a pyro-

the possibility of the configuration of more effective models, capable of combating enemy threats into the first years of the next century.

Among its basic qualities is its straightforward usage (the shooter only needs to aim the reticule of the telescope, center it on the target and fire), and a computer that is in charge of making the necessary corrections

THE FRENCH ARMÉE DE TERRE

The anti-tank attack helicopters of the French army have double HOT missile stands capable of hitting the heaviest targets up to 14,100 feet away; this distance is attained by taking advantage of the momentum of the aircraft during the launch.

technic fuse, or a double blank charge with a laser fuse on the HOT 3 that provokes electrical ignition, even if initiated on terrain angled at more than 65°; the charge doesn't activate until the weapon is 98.5 to 165 feet from the launcher and the parts that guide it. The guiding system is composed of: a thermal battery that is activated when the missile is fired and supplies the necessary electrical energy during the flight; a decoder that receives signals from the telecommand and transmits them to the jet deflector; a gyroscope that gives the position of the missile; the stabilizing module; a guiding cable spooled around the weapon so that it unwinds as it advances; and two infrared transmitters that follow the missile's trajectory during the day or at night.

Great destructive capacity

Incredibly resistant to various methods of counterattack and capable of attacking two targets in less than a minute, the HOT stands out from equivalent systems for its high penetration capability. This has been proved time and time again: from the war in the Falklands, where British helicopters were armed with it, to Operation Peace for Galilee, where the Syrians fired more than a hundred of these systems against Israeli armored tanks and transport and personnel vehicles.

THE ENEMY TANK

Anti-tank missiles are one of the biggest threats to combat tanks. The Spanish BO-105 helicopters of the BHELA 1 are amazingly effective in this regard; they incorporate two triple batteries of HOT missiles that can penetrate the most advanced shields.

EASY TO USE

This diagram of the process of launching from HOT air launch pads shows how straightforward it is, since the weapons operator only has to keep the target centralized in the viewfinder; the calculations and corrections are done automatically.

This destructive capacity was due to the blank penetrating charge of the type HEAT in the first two versions of the HOT, and the double charge in tandem in model 3. This last model is activated by a short-range laser fuse, which detonates the second charge at the ideal moment to take advantage of the first charge's damage to the armor. The probability of impact against fixed targets of 90.5 × 90.5 inches or moving ones of 90.5 × 181 inches is 80 %, if they are located less than 1,640 feet away, and close to 100 % for longer distances; its military operators have a success rate of close to 90 %.

The truth about its penetration capacity is a jealously guarded secret, although it is known that the approximately 8.82 pounds of

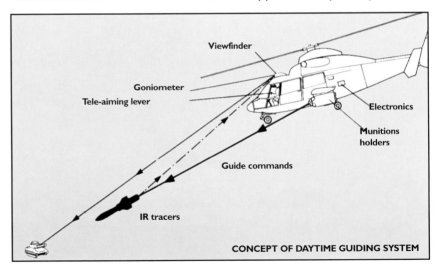

CONCEPT OF DAYTIME GUIDING SYSTEM

explosives in the active charge are able to penetrate an armored mass of between 31.5 and 42 inches depending on the model. With regard to spaced out targets, it can pierce a triple target of NATO heavyweight tanks, including three armored plates from 4 to 31.5 inches situated at an angle of 65° with respect to the horizontal line of separation between them; the impact uses residual energy in order to continue penetrating 7.88 inches of metal sheets located 9.85 feet from the last one. It may also be used, if necessary, against secondary targets such as casemates or enemy weapons.

Aiming and guiding equipment

Although the location of the aiming and guiding elements depends on the set-up, their basic configuration includes an optical view-finder, which may be part of the tower or turn independently. In addition, there is an infrared locator parallel to the aiming optic with a wide search range of 2.5° during the first three seconds of flight, and a narrow field of 0.5° during the cruising phase. The latter works with an electronic device that sends the missile any signals necessary to change its line of fire.

At present, the system has an electronic guiding system that uses past signals to produce the commands it sends to the missile to situate it back on the line of fire. It also includes some compartments that provide services to complete the installation: interconnection and autocontrol, command and

ATLAS LIGHTWEIGHT STAND
Small Acmat trucks can be set up to transport long-range anti-tank systems by attaching the monotube launch stand and the reloading containers in the back. The bodywork of this vehicle has received total armored protection.

selection of munitions, and the firing circuit with an activator that induces firing. It should be pointed out that the different launch stands normally transport one or several munitions in firing position, which are automatically connected to the firing circuit so they can be activated when necessary. The reloading process may carried out with the help of the automatic systems or manually.

THE MISSILE LAUNCH
This image shows the moment a HOT missile leaves the launch-container tube at the side of a Gazelle helicopter to move toward the signaled point of impact; the weapon is resistant to countermeasures and can hit two different 'targets in less than a minute.

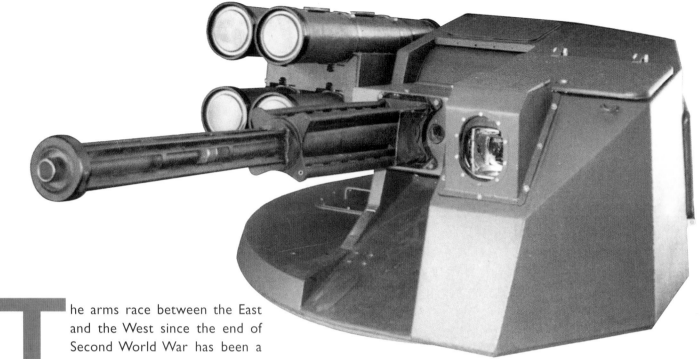

The arms race between the East and the West since the end of Second World War has been a major influence on most of the weapons systems developed and used up to now, including various Soviet models of tanks and armored vehicles.

With the aim of supporting the advance of their own troops and blocking that of the enemy armored formations, several generations of anti-tank missiles were designed and exported to satellite states, in keeping with the former Soviet Union's policy of arms sales. These models were used to consolidate a powerful industry and validate design concepts that are now in production. The missiles have a level of technology and capacity pretty similar to their Western counterparts, but their cost is less.

ONE PERSON TURRET

The Kliver is a turret that can be installed in various types of wheeled and chained vehicles. A 30 millimeter automatic cannon has been installed on it, as well as a machine gun that measures 7.62 mm, and a quadruple stand for long-range anti-tank missiles, which are controlled by the incorporated guiding system.

LONG-RANGE SYSTEM

The Kornet-E is an anti-tank missile launcher that can hit targets at a distance of 18,050 feet from the firing mechanism. It incorporates a semi-automatic laser guiding system that makes its destruction by defense troops difficult.

In production since the 1970's

The first known model of anti-tank missile developed for the former Soviet army was the wire-guided 3M6 "Smell" —bumblebee— which NATO called the AT-1 SNAPPER. It was a rudimentary weapon in terms of design and performance. It had a range of 7,550 feet, achieved via a manual guiding system used by the system operator. In general, it was launched from quadruple stands installed in light UAZ-69 vehicles or the armored reconnaissance vehicles, BRDM-1.

A generation tested in combat

In 1965, to complement the SNAPPER, production was begun on the 9M17 "Scorpion" known as the AT-2 SWATTER. It was different from the other in that it included a guiding system by UHF radio, which was very useful for launches from Mi-24 HIND attack helicopters, as long as the wires didn't get caught in the treetops. Nevertheless, its advanced penetration capability —which allowed it to pierce a steel plate of 480 millimeters in thickness at a maximum distance of about 8,200 feet proved very vulnerable to electronic interference. It also had a high firing distance if the fuse wasn't armed until the missile had traveled 1,640 feet from the launch point.

Widely exported to various countries in the East and Middle East, with stands for helicopters or BRMD-1 vehicles, its distribution was parallel to that of the portable wire-guided 9M14 "Malyutka" or AT-3 SAGGER. This system eclipsed many of the qualities of the old one because it was the weapon used by the Egyptians in 1973 to annihilate the Israeli armored formations during the conflict in the Suez Canal. It has been said that it destroyed as many as 85 tanks in three and a half minutes.

One year previous, the North Vietnamese had used the system to destroy some of the South Vietnamese Army's armor-plated vehicles. In 1973, the Syrians also used it, although with little success. More recently, it has been deployed by the Iraqis in the Gulf War and the separatists in the former Yugoslavia.

Easy to use and maneuver

The SAGGER –which includes the wire-guided optical A variant, the B with an improved engine that allows for more speed, and the C with a semiautomatic guiding system introduced at the end of the 1970's—has been successfully sold in about twenty countries.

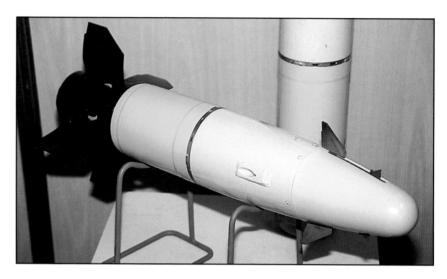

EXPORTED ACROSS THE WORLD
The anti-tank systems offered at a good price by the defense industries of Russia, the Ukraine and other ex-Soviet republics are being purchased by Asian and Middle Eastern countries that want to improve their capacity to neutralize modern combat tanks.

Among them are Algeria, China and Taiwan, where they produce unlicensed copies, Cuba, India, Libya, Poland, Hungary, Vietnam and South Yemen.

Among its most significant features is the fact that it can be used from a lightweight launch pad, from a vehicle or launched from a helicopter. The ground pad consists of a control mechanism and two missiles transported by three men; the one for vehicles is a sextuplet stand that can be attached to all BRDM vehicles or a rail located above the main gun of BMP-1 combat vehicles. It can also be launched

AUTOMATIC LASER GUIDE
Ex-Soviet designers are working on new plans for missiles to detect a laser beam which would direct them toward the assigned target, or providing them with a self-searching mechanism that would localize the points assigned by the operator.

TECHNICAL CHARACTERISTICS OF THE KORNET-E ANTI-TANK MISSILE

COST IN DOLLARS:	Varies with each client	PERFORMANCE:	
DIMENSIONS:		Range	From 330 to 18,050 feet during the day and up to 11,500 at night
Length	47.28 in	Speed	Subsonic
Diameter	6 in	Flying time	20 seconds to reach its maximum range
WEIGHT:		Penetration	About 2,630 feet
Launcher	55 lbs	**LAUNCH PADS:**	From ground in tripod or in vehicular stands
Missile container	64 lbs		
Missile	55 lbs	**PROBABILITY OF IMPACT:**	90 %
Thermal camera	24 lbs		
PROPULSION:			
Rocket engine with four fins at the tail and two in front to control the flight			

from all types of aircraft ranging from the heavy Mi-8 "Hip" to the light SA 342 "Gazelle".

The improved model has a probability of impact in excess of 90 %, a range of 9,850 feet, and weighs 24 pounds at launch time. In addition, it is equipped with a blank charge in its warhead that can penetrate almost twenty inches of steel, and improved features such as a forward extension for the optimal detonation of the missile head.

Second generation models

The fact that the Soviets were behind, technologically speaking, in comparison to the West

NIGHTTIME GUIDING MODULE

The compact thermal camera works well and is easy to use; it was designed to launch the new generation of anti-tank missiles, developed in Soviet research institutes, at any time of the day or night.

meant that it wasn't until 1975 that the new 9KIII "Fagot" or At-4 SPIGOT was developed. This system was very much like the French/German MILAN in its configuration and features.

This system incorporates missiles in cylindrical containers, which facilitates their launch from a lightweight stand with a tripod maneuvered by two operators, and semiautomatic guiding equipment; it has a range of 1.2 miles. In 1982, it was used by the Syrians, and Israel captured some units, which helped the Western secret services to become more familiar with the details of a system that had also been

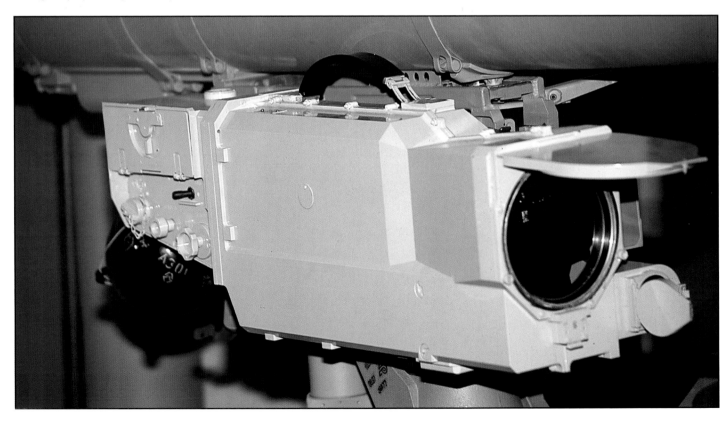

installed on an individual stand on the BMP-2 and BDM-2.

The designs become more and more capable

During the procession in Red Square in 1977, an anti-tank missile system composed of a battery of five containers installed in a modified variant of the BRDM-2 vehicle was presented; it looked very much like the HOT. Shortly after, it was discovered that the system was the AT-5 SPANDREL with a destructive capacity of up to 13,130 feet, a powerful penetration capability of about 750 mm, and a semiautomatic guiding system commanded by infrared transmitters at the rear of the weapon.

The 9M114 "Kokon" or the AT-6 SPIRAL was developed to equip helicopters with a more capable model, and the first units armed the Mi-24 "Hind-E" helicopters stationed in Germany in 1978. With an estimated range of about 5 miles and an advanced guiding system (with no need of a wire to transmit orders to the missile during the flight), the missile had an elongated shape with small fins at the tail to carry out the necessary changes in the direction of attack. Subsequently, a newly designed variant was introduced called the AT-9 SHTURM.

A new system called the 9M120 "Vikhr" or AT-12 was produced in Tula by KPB to arm various types of aircraft such as Ka-50/52 "Black Shark" helicopters and Su-25 "Frogfoot" attack planes. It is characterized by its

ARMAMENT OF THE "BLACK" HELICOPTER

The 9M120 "Vikhr" or AT-12 long-range anti-tank missile includes a laser guiding system and has a range of 6.2 miles. It weights 130 lbs, and a helicopter can transport up to 16 of them.

LONG-RANGE MISSILES

This battery of eight anti-tank missiles installed on the Mil Mi-28 "Havoc" Russian attack helicopter is a significant indication of the superior destructive capability of these air methods against armored formations.

guiding system via a laser command channel. It has a range of 6.2 miles and penetrates 40 inches of steel thanks to its explosive head with a blank charge activated by a mixed close-range or impact fuse. It weighs 130 lbs inside its container and only takes 14 seconds to travel 19,700 feet from the launch point; thus it can fire a round of two missiles at the same target.

The latest model, intended to be launched from the air, is the 9M120/121 or AT-16; at the moment, there is a lack of any real information on its performance, although Soviet export companies offer it to potential clients interested in the most advanced technology.

Other models fight over a limited market

In spite of the change in the exportation policies of countries like Russia and the Ukraine, who offer their products at a very competitive price, the reality is that the market is monopolized by systems developed in Europe and the U.S. However, the proposed systems include various models of thermal cameras like the "Mulat-115", with a weight of only 11 lbs, to be used by the "Metis" and "Metis-M" systems or the "Fagot" and "Konkurs-M" systems. They are now updating a model, the IPN79 "Metis-2", that is intended for the "Kornet-E and TP" or may be installed on the stand of the short-range missile "Pantsyr-SI".

The "Kornet", manufactured by KBP, is a new system with launchers for the infantry,

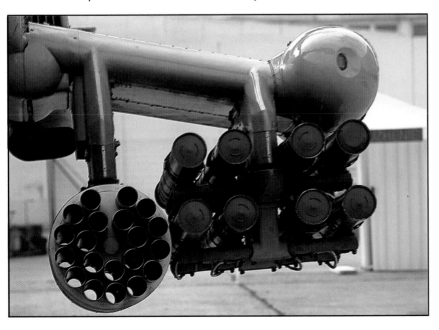

stands for light vehicles, quadruple stands attached to the Kliver turret, which can be used to arm various types of armor-plated vehicles, and double stands with automatic reloading for caterpillar tracks. Used by the Russian Armed Forces, this system has a range of 18,050 feet during the day, and 11,500 at night. It can be equipped with a head with two blank charges in tandem or one multi-purpose charge, and is the only one of its kind on the market with a semiautomatic laser guiding system. In addition, its launcher weighs 55 lbs, the missile in its container is 64 lbs, and the thermal camera is 24 lbs.

Other weapons guided by this new design include a small missile of 100 mm in diameter and another of 125 mm. They are designed to be fired from the bore of Soviet combat tanks and can hit targets at a distance of 16,400 feet thanks to their semiautomatic laser guiding system –the same one used by the "Kilotov-2M" projectile that is fired from artillery stands against objectives situated at a distance of 9.3 miles.

VEHICULAR LAUNCH

The armored caterpillar tracks of the BMP series incorporate a rail at the rear end of the main cannon to hold medium-range anti-tank missiles, which are guided by the system attached to the viewfinder (on the right side of the photo).

EVOLUTIONARY DESIGN

The photo shows one of the new generation of Soviet anti-tank missiles, in black, with its steering and stabilizing fins deployed. This system represents a substantial technological improvement over past models.

Land Rovers, British off-road vehicles, have been used in a variety of configurations and models over the last century and have witnessed a good number of military and peaceful interventions between the armies of many nations.

The Moroccan desert, the Congolese steppe, the beaches of Spain and Italy, the Malaysian jungle and the mountainous regions of Scotland are some of the arenas where this vehicle has proven its capacity for movement —crossing flowing rivers, driving through muddy areas or climbing steep slopes that similar models (some much more modern) would get stuck on.

Production arises out of a post-military necessity

British finances and industrial capacity were seriously damaged after the Second World War, and many manufacturers affected a policy of adaptability to overcome the crisis.

The Rover company, producer of a wide range of private cars until that time, decided

RATIONAL INSTRUMENTS
Military use requires that the vehicular instruments function even in the most adverse weather conditions, where the treatment or maintenance of the vehicle is not favorable.

DEEP RIVERS
The infantry units of the Marines, such as these British Royal Marines, are equipped with Land Rovers which are able to cross deep rivers.

to undertake several projects that would allow it to maintain its business. Among its past projects was a four-wheel-drive vehicle, characterized by a light alloy bodywork that adapted to the shortage of steel. Unveiled in 1948 at the Auto Exposition in Amsterdam, it sold very well, and in two years, 24,000 units had been sold with bodywork made from aluminum.

Military sales are initiated in the British Army

The interest of British military representatives in the Land Rover commenced at the same time its reputation for capacity and performance was growing, and in 1956, they adopted Model 88 as a standardized 1/4 ton vehicle. Its use in armies and maneuvers, particularly with other countries, had a favorable effect on its success, and it was subsequently adopted by several NATO countries and armed forces under British influence.

Operational experience led to work on another military model with a cargo capacity of 3/4 ton, designated as Model 109.

Some of these models were modified to transport the armored vehicle crews that patrolled Belfast, were attacks against troops deployed there were continuous. Others were modified as command posts, mobile radar surveillance along the coast, desert patrol vehicles, etc. There was even a semi-caterpillar track variant called Centaur, whose back end was adapted to the wheel assembly of the light Scorpion tank.

These variants, each one improving on the last in terms of performance and adaptation to military use, maintained the production line active, satisfying Britain's own needs and those of other countries interested in the products. These included Saudi Arabia, Australia, Belgium, Spain, Holland, Japan, Indonesia, Ireland, Jamaica, Kenya, Libya, Malaysia,

SIMPLE INTERIOR
The Land Rovers produced under military specifications have a simple interior. This includes very resistant canvas seats that are comfortable enough so that the driver and his assistant can travel without difficulty. Also, the gearshift and the instruments are very accessible.

Morocco, Sudan, Turkey, Zaire, Zambia and Zimbabwe; some of these countries have permits to produce them in their own factories. Those produced in Spain have been exported to Egypt and Morocco.

Copyright Metalúrgica de Santa Ana, S.A.

In the mid 1950's, an agreement was signed between the British company and the Spanish firm SANTANA, authorizing them to produce various models in the Land Rover range. As a result of this agreement, the production of models destined for the civilian

TECHNICAL CHARACTERISTICS OF THE LAND ROVER DEFENDER 90

COST IN DOLLARS:	3,000,000		Gas tank capacity	54.5 l
DIMENSIONS:			**PROPULSION:**	
Length	146.65 in		A wide range of gasoline and diesel engines between 68 and 134 hp	
Height	78.52 in		**PERFORMANCE:**	
Width	70.53 in		Longitudinal gradient	70 %
Ground clearance	9.02 in with 7.50 x 16 tires		Turn radius	226.5 in
WEIGHT:			Depth of crossed body of water	0.197 in
Empty	5,300 lbs with standard suspension		Angle of approximation	51°
Maximum	7,940 lbs		Angle of departure	52°
Maximum cargo	2,285 lbs		Range	From 310 to 500 miles depending on engine and fuel used
Cargo in tow	1,100 lbs off-road and up to 8,820 lbs on the road			

sector began in 1956; models designed for military use were also produced, among them Model 109, which was used by the Spanish Army as well as the Marines.

Then a lighter model was configured, which received several changes to its bodywork and the location of some of the components. Among its basic features was the fact that it was 4x4, could transport up to 8 men or 2,200 lbs of cargo, and was powered (in the latest versions) by a diesel engine with 91.7 hp. Many of these units are still being used by the Spanish Army as evacuation ambulances, recovery vehicles, weapons platforms or mobile communications posts.

To complement this last model, production was begun in the beginning of the 1970's on Model 88, designed to transport 1,100 lbs or up to six men.

The light version has become very popular for its ability to cross all types of terrain, its sturdiness and resistance, and the fact that it can be launched by parachute into the battle zone. It is also configured as a platform to transport M40A1 non-recoiling cannons, lightweight launchers from the MILAN missile system, or it can be armed with various types of machine guns. Among its most

MILITARY AND ROBUST

The lighter Land Rover 109 has proven very sturdy and capable during the twenty years it has been used by the Spanish army. The photo shows the part in the front of the vehicle that enables it to be towed by other vehicles.

GREAT MOBILITY

The Land Rover 109 is capable of transporting up to 2,200 lbs of cargo or eight men, or (as shown in the photo) it can tow objects weighing half a ton. It has no problems moving artillery pieces of almost two tons during relocation procedures.

important features is its weight without cargo of 3,660 lbs and diesel engine with 59 hp; it is also easy to maneuver and requires little logistical maintenance.

The Defender series, models with updated performance features

In 1984, production began on the 90 series, which incorporated substantial advances such as disk brakes in the front axle and an improved long distance suspension. Work was also begun to develop a model capable of competing with the new off-road vehicles being offered on the market by various manufacturers; a majority of them were adapta-

tions of civilian vehicles that had been produced during the sales explosion of this type of automobile in many Western countries.

Model 90, light and capable

The British Armed Forces needed to update their supply of light off-road vehicles with a model that would satisfy the requirements of the TUL program (Truck, Utility, Light); they decided that the Defender 90 fulfilled their necessities for transporting personnel by towing lightweight flat beds with one axle. In addition, the model was ideal for transporting certain types of lightweight weapons systems that were too heavy to be carried by the infantry.

This model can transport the driver, two people in the front seat, and four in the back, who can use the comfortable seats and benches by entering through the two side doors or the tailgate. It is extremely mobile in all types of situations as it has four-wheel-drive, a manual gear shift box with four forward gears and one in reverse, a suspension with shock absorbing springs, and a gasoline or diesel engine. There are several models ranging from a diesel engine with 2.5 liters and 68 hp to a V-8 gasoline one with 3.528 liters and 134 hp.

In addition, its front headlights are built into the bodywork and protected by metal grilles. It can incorporate a winch in the rear

SEVERAL ROOFS

The large platform of the Land Rover can be adopted for a wide variety of uses; in particular, the format of the roof can be changed to store various types of equipment in the interior. It can also tow additional equipment with a lightweight hook.

A LARGE VARIETY OF USES

The Land Rover's ability to maneuver over all types of terrain means it has been used in a wide range of missions. There are Military Police models with non-recoiling guns, or configurations of ambulances, cisterns, tanks, or general cargo.

for use in difficult situations; the spare tire is anchored to the hood. It can also have a canvas convertible top, held in place by metal supports, or a watertight roof for protection from inclement weather.

The 110 has more cargo capacity

This Land Rover was used by the British Armed Forces during Operation Granby to liberate Kuwait from Iraqi occupation. It is known as the TUM (Truck, Utility, Medium). The current model of the Defender series has been updated from one produced in 1983 and incorporates a 110 inch chassis; this measurement is also the vehicle's designation.

Its general configuration stays true to many others of the company's designs and incorporates an elongated chassis with four tractor wheels. The engine is located in the front and is easy to get to because of the large hood. The driver and two more men can sit up front, and up to 10 people can travel in the back. It can transport a maximum cargo

This model is powered by an Isuzu 4BDIT 3.9 liter turbodiesel engine with 121 hp. The Land Rover 110 Heavy Duty variant, developed for the Australians, also uses this engine; more than 400 units of this model have been manufactured.

It has a double rear wheel assembly, making it a 6x6. It has a large cargo capacity, which has allowed for the development of a variant for 12 people or an ambulance with six stretchers. In addition, the standard versions can travel 370 miles, and a reconnaissance convoy specified for special troops can go 620 miles.

of 3,280 lbs, and can tow 1,100 lbs over all types of terrain and up to 8,820 lbs on the road.

Variants of this model have been manufactured with open tops, such as those used by reconnaissance patrols of the British Special Air Service (SAS). These are also being armed with machine guns and rocket launchers and with closed tops; they are designed for use in all types of missions such as controlling vehicles by remote control or transporting LAU-97 70 millimeter multiple rocket launchers. It has an 80 liter gas tank, which gives it a long range. The front is designed with an angle of attack of 50° to confront the various things that may block its path. All of these features had a decisive impact on the Australian Army's decision to buy it.

Close to three thousand of these have been produced with a permit in the Moorebank factory in New Wales.

TACTICAL COMMUNICATIONS

The Mercurio, Centauro and Tritón systems, part of the tactical communication unit of the Spanish Army, can be transported and maneuvered from modified Land Rover vehicles. These incorporate a rear waterproof cabin where the operators can work more comfortably and are protected from inclement weather.

In the last several decades, the Spanish Ministry of Defense's policy of buying military products has favored the acquisition of those items manufactured by factory's in Spain over the, sometime, more rational and economical, purchase of those produced in other countries. This policy led the representatives of the purchasing board of the Dirección General de Armamento y Material (DGAM) to call for proposals on developing a chassis that could transport 1,100 lbs of cargo over all types of terrain; this would substitute older models such as the Ebro-Viasa C3J and some Land Rovers 88. The following year, they requested proposals on developing a vehicle capable of transporting double the weight, in order to replace Dodge trucks and Land Rovers 109.

Spanish factory same chosen

The features of the technical specifications that governed each proposal —developed without further delay after being organized a year apart— motivated the selection of two Spanish companies. These were the Industria Metalúrgica Santa Ana —which pro-

posed the development of a model based on the experience of manufacturing several series of Land Rovers —and Nissan, a Japanese firm that had recently acquired Motor Ibérica— who planned to transform the civilian model, Patrol.

Extensive testing on both models

To verify that they performed as proposed, a commission of military experts was formed to check how the technical features of the vehicles adapted to their requirements; the testing also took into account other tactical and economical necessities.

Two prototypes of each of the vehicles were submitted to a general examination during which they checked the serial numbers, the measurements, the weights, the volume of the lubricants, and the fulfillment of the technical requirements. Then the performance was checked: testing the engine on slopes, revising the brake system, checking the velocity and acceleration, and examining the vehicles' capacity to cross rivers and pass over longitudinal and transversal gradients.

Then the resistance and fuel consumption tests took place, using the maximum cargo of each variant over a distance of approximately 6,200 miles —four cycles of 1,550 miles each. The maximum duration of each cycle was about two weeks. During this time, it was driven over asphalt highways, paved roads,

mountain paths, and rolling, wet and marshy land. The tests were very rigorous as far as fulfilling the specifications, and the process was finalized with an extensive revision of the mechanical elements to check the wear and tear and state of operation.

The Japanese option

The Nissan Patrol models —MC-4 (Military Short) and ML-6 (Military Long)— that successfully passed the tests were nothing more than modified civilian vehicles. They had been given various external touch-ups to fulfill their "militarization" such as modifying some STANAG with regard to their various components and accessories.

At first, the Spanish military was unenthusiastic about both models as they had been shown to be less robust than those they were substituting and hadn't fulfilled some requirements such as those for front and rear ground clearance. In spite of this, models began arriving for the troops in large batches. At present, several thousands of

TRANSPORTATION OF WEAPONS
The Nissan ML-6 vehicles used by the Spanish Paratrooper Brigade have been modified to transport the MILAN anti-tank missile system. They have also been incorporated with various nets to camouflage them when they are in firing position.

them continue to be used by the Spanish Army, Air Force, Navy, and the local and state police. Models following similar designs have been manufactured for the British and Algerian Armed Forces.

General features of the vehicle

The Nissan factory, in Zona Franca in Barcelona, is where the parts from other factories or the suppliers are assembled. The

bodywork and the chassis are welded together by robots, making them very resistant; then they pass through a plant where they are given an anticorrosive protective covering and a layer of paint that protects them from atmospheric agents; finally, the various mechanical elements are assembled.

Vehicle adapted to military use

The bodywork is made from anodized steel and given a coat of paint treated with an anti-infrared agent. It is a portable vehicle, and is joined to the chassis via elastic supports that isolate it from vibrations. It incorporates a curved windshield that goes to the hood and a removable safety framework that protects the interior of the vehicle in case it overturns.

Both models are provided with a hook for towing in the center of the back end and incorporate two robust steel bumpers. They are equipped with a diesel engine that, in the case of the MC-4, is an A4 with 2.8 liters and 88.6 hp; in the case of the ML-6, the engine is a SD33 with 3.2 liters and 95 hp. These vehicles include engines connected to a manual gearbox with five forward gears and one reverse, cooling by circulation of water, and lubrication via a closed circuit of oil pressure.

> **SPECIAL MODIFICATION**
>
> The Spanish Marines' necessity for a specific variant of the Patrol MC-4, which could transport M40A1 106 millimeter non-recoiling cannons, called for a redesigned model with an interesting double system of pulling down the windshield.

> **CIVILIAN DESIGN AND MILITARY USE**
>
> Nissan Patrol military vehicles are adaptations of the civilian models with the necessary changes for their new use.

In case of war, they use a NATO reduced light circuit that essentially effects the front headlights, position lights and brake lights. When driving at night, a system of ultraviolet illumination is used and, for reading maps, the driver's assistant has an auxiliary light in the cab that is difficult to detect from the exterior.

The capacity of the MC-4 allows for transportation of the driver and his assistant in the two front seats and four more soldiers on the benches in the cargo hold. The ML-6 can transport up to ten men in the back. The MC-4 can move 1,545 pounds of cargo and the ML-6 2,205; both can tow 1,655 pounds and incorporate hooks that facilitate their loading and unloading from ships or aircraft.

Models to satisfy a variety of requirements

The vehicle has a competitive price of around 25,000 dollars per unit. The need to maintain the activity of the factory and its jobs and some political pressures have led to the manufacturing of all types of units, from combat to logistical. Currently, new variants based on the basic vehicle are being produced. They are armor-plated so as to operate in highly dangerous zones, and amphibious, outfitted with equipment that enables them to drive along the beachhead without water entering the engine. There are variants to carry shelters for special communications teams, models to transport M40A1 106mm

non-recoiling cannons (with a redesigned front windshield), half-top ambulances with two stretchers and medical equipment, light-weight cisterns with 1,000 liter vats, and units that transport anti-air systems such as those used by the EADA to move the Atlas-Mistral. They can also be used as combat vehicles with stands for medium and heavyweight machine guns, LAG-40 40 millimeter automatic grenade launchers, and medium and long-range anti-tank missile launchers.

ARMORED POLICE VEHICLES
The Rural Anti-terrorist Group (GAR) of the Spanish state police move around in the Short Nissan Patrol with armor-plating over all its bodywork and windows to protect the agents in case of a terrorist attack.

MILITARIZED CIVILIAN VEHICLES
This Patrol ML-6 is one of the vehicles used by the Spanish legionaries. The spare tire has been moved to the roof of the bodywork, and there has been a sign posted on the front to warn drivers of the presence of a military vehicle.

DRIVER'S SEAT

The personnel who drive these military vehicles say that they are easy to maneuver and comfortable while on the road. The instrument panel has been transformed for military use.

CANVAS TOP

Military use of these vehicles requires the cargo hold to be covered by a canvas top to protect it from dust. The top and its hooks can be disassembled easily.

CARGO CAPACITY

The cargo hold is in the rear. It is accessed by the tailgate, and inside there are two benches for four men, the spare tire, and space for the radio equipment.

TOW HOOK

In the center of the rear bumper, there is a standard NATO tow hook. It can tow weights of 750 kilograms over all types of terrain and up to 1,700 kg on asphalt roads.

FRONT SEATS

The driver and his assistant are provided with comfortable seats covered with canvas to make them more resistant to military use.

TECHNICAL CHARACTERISTICS OF THE NISSAN PATROL MC-4

COST IN DOLLARS:	25,000,000		Gas tank capacity	82 l
DIMENSIONS:			**PROPULSION:**	
Length	161.74 in		SD 33 4 cylinder Nissan diesel engine with 2.82 l and 84 hp	
Height	77.62 in		at 3,600 r.p.m.	
Width	66.59 in		**PERFORMANCE:**	
Ground clearance	8.67 in		Longitudinal gradient	110 %
WEIGHT:			Transversal gradient	43 %
Empty	3,970 lbs		Depth of crossed body of water	23.64 in
Maximum	5,500 lbs		Maximum speed	78 mph
Maximum cargo	1,545 lbs		Range	500 miles
Cargo in tow	1,655 lbs without brakes			
	3,750 lbs with brakes			

FOLDING WINDSHIELD

A strange and inefficient system of metal hooks allows the front windshield to be folded down on the hood, reducing the general height of the vehicle. This is done using the handle at the bottom of the windshield.

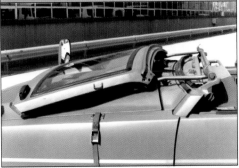

LARGE MIRRORS

In order to see around blind spots, the driver has the use of two large collapsible mirrors situated at the far front on the fender.

FRONT AREA

The MC-4 incorporates a sturdy bumper at the front to protect it from impacts. The headlights are built into the bodywork and covered with a protective grille.

WEAPONS LAUNCH PAD
HUMMER off-road vehicles have excellent tactical mobility and good strategic capacity. They can serve as excellent launch pads for various weapons systems, such as the TOW anti-tank missile launcher.

The mediocre performances of the enormous fleet of light off-road vehicles used by the U.S. Army until the end of the 1970's led to the development of a new model with superior features adapted to the current necessities of the world's armies. In addition, it has the innate qualities to become the vehicle against which all the models presently on the market are measured.

DESERT COMBAT
On the occasion of U.S. participation in the Gulf War, some HUMMER vehicles were modified to improve their capability in the desert; they were equipped with many cases of water and extra fuel and were painted so that they blended in with their surroundings.

The HUMMER —as this off-road vehicle is popularly known— has been used in deserts, steep areas, beaches and the Alaskan tundra; in all these places, it has responded gracefully to the challenges of driving in such adverse conditions. This has led to its integration into the U.S. Armed Forces. In addition, it has been purchased by various countries wishing to enhance the capacity for movement and combat of their own land and amphibious units.

Smooth and rapid development

In 1980, the U.S Army Tank and Automotive Command (TACOM) began preliminary research on developing the general design of a new light off-road vehicle to replace the current models. The program, called HMMWV (High Mobility Multipurpose Wheeled Vehicle), was begun in 1981. A total of 61 companies submitted proposals, and those belonging to AM General, Chrysler and

Teledyne Continental were chosen.

The designs present advanced solutions

The 11 prototypes presented by each one were submitted to tests at the Nevada Automotive Test Center to verify their features and performance. The vehicles were driven a total of 13,050 miles under the strict control of various measuring instruments.

On 22 March 1983, the HUMMER (High Utility Maximum Mobility Easy Rider), designed by AM General, was chosen, and 2,344 units of the M998.A variant were contracted. That order was followed by others, bringing the total to 54,973 units and 1,200 million dollars. Production was initiated at the Mishawaka factory in Indiana at the beginning of 1983, and 39,000 units went to the army. The rest were divided equally between the navy, the air force and the marines. The good results obtained by their operational deployment led to new orders, raising the number of units produced for the U.S. Armed Forces to 10,000. These have replaced other models, such as the Jeep M151, the Mechanical Mule M274, the Gama Goat M792 and vehicles in the M880 series.

Its reputation leads to high export sales

The joint participation of U.S troops with those in several other countries made the superior qualities of the HUMMER known and led to export contracts for 10,000 units to around thirty countries, including Abu

EQUIPEMENT FOR CROSSING RIVERS

The canvas covering on the cargo hold of this HUMMER identifies it as one of the units assigned to transport medium cargo. This model has an inlet tube on the left side to protect the engine when fording deep rivers.

OPTIMIZED FOR COMBAT

Its design qualities, superior performance, and ability to accomplish a wide variety of tactical missions make the HUMMER a very useful tool in all types of combat situations.

Dhabi, Saudi Arabia, Djibouti, the Philippines, Qatar, Luxembourg, Mexico, Thailand and Taiwan. In addition, orders came from governmental organizations such as the Chinese Ministry of Oil Mining and the U.S Border Patrol.

Another country that uses these excellent tactical vehicles is Spain, which purchased two hundred for the infantry regiment of the navy (TEAR) to use during amphibious vehicle landings. They have been proven to be ideal for the transport of men, moving weapons systems, evacuating the injured or performing logistical missions. They have also been used in Bosnia in peacekeeping missions.

Remarkable mechanical configuration

The HUMMER is a light vehicle designed to transport up to 2,535 pounds or tow cargo or systems weighing up to 3,300 pounds. To do this, it has been equipped with four-wheel-drive, which enables it to drive over the most rugged terrain.

Its basic configuration can hold the driver and three more people seated comfortably in individual seats. It is easy to get into due to the large side doors, which can be easily dismantled if necessary.

Powerful and highly mobile

Under the hood, there is a very powerful

increases or decreases the tire pressure in relation to the terrain they are traveling over.

The available power is enough to reach a maximum speed of 70 miles per hour. It is capable of driving up 60 % longitudinal gradients, traversing 40 % gradients and fording rivers and other bodies of water up to 30 inches; this increases to 40 inches with the aid of a tube on the right side of the vehicle, visible from the exterior, which provides the engine with air.

For optimum performance, the chassis has been designed to take up the entire length of the vehicle and is made up of two sturdy carbon steel crossbeams. The suspension system consists of four double oscillating arms, fixed to the chassis, and joined to the road wheels. The front and rear torsion bars help to stabilize the vehicle. The bodywork of the vehicle is made of aluminum and reinforced with steel and other synthetic materials, reducing its empty weight to 5,327 pounds.

General Motors diesel engine with eight cylinders that, in the first model, is 6.2 liters with 130 hp and, in the current model, increases to 150 hp. This excellent engine is joined to an automatic gearbox with three forward gears and one reverse and another box, which supplies complete traction with the help of the incorporation of the CTIS system (Central Tire Inflation System). This system

OPERATIONAL CAPACITY

The design of the HUMMER incorporates a lot of details that make it ideal for military use. The photo shows how its doors can be removed when the outside temperature is so high that it is uncomfortable to be inside it.

It has a height of 49 inches, which signifi-

USED BY THE MARINES

The U.S. marines use several thousand of these excellent off-road vehicles, capable of carrying out a wide variety of missions. This is a reconnaissance model, equipped with a heavy M-2 machine gun measuring 12.70 x 99 mm.

ce with space for four patients in stretchers or eight sitting up; the M1035A2, a soft-top ambulance; the M1113 with a more powerful engine of 190 hp for use in special missions that require more speed or heavier cargo; and the M1114 and M1116 variants manufactured by O'Gara-Hess & Eisenhardt. This last model is capable of stopping light arms fire; the U.S. Air Force has already purchased 71 units.

cantly reduces its appearance, and a width of 86 inches, which improves its stability. It can travel about 350 miles thanks to the 95 liters of diesel the shockproof gas tank can hold. With four flat tires, it can travel 30 miles at a maximum speed of 30 mph.

COMBAT METHOD

This variant of the HUMMER armed with armor-plating on its bodywork and windows can be used during combat when limited fire is predicted, and a powerful vehicle is needed to complete the mission.

Designs developed to carry out specific jobs

The initial contract already had in mind the production of 15 basic variants. These have been continuously produced since the current series was put on the market; it is called A1 and incorporates a more solid chassis, among other things. To date, more than 140,000 units have been produced, and more are planned with the introduction of the A2 model, which has a diesel engine with 6.5 liters and 160 hp.

The initial standard model M998 for the transportation of personnel —which continues to be produced in its A2 version— and its variants have been replaced by eight basic models and their civilian variants.

The military models also include the M1097A2, which is offered in four configurations to transport troops, cargo or shelters; the M1025A2 with a stand that can hold weapons ranging from a medium-weight machine gun to a TOW guided missile launcher; the M1043A2 and M1045A2, modifications of the M1025A2 with improved armor-plating; the M997A2, configured as a protected ambulan-

EXPLORATION AND RECONNAISSANCE

The infantry squads assigned to patrol the front lines use the HUMMER for its capacity to move over all types of terrain and the many possibilities it offers for transporting personnel.

CARGO HOLD

The cargo hold of the HUMMER is accessible through a large upper door and a smaller tailgate; this transports the personal equipment of the soldiers and their assigned weapons. It has four-wheel-drive, which enables it to drive over rugged terrain. Its basic configuration has space for a driver and three more people seated in comfortable individual seats. Its large side door makes for easy access and may be easily taken apart if necessary.

TOP HATCH

On the top of the HUMMER, there is a hatch, which protects the operator when he is using a weapon inside it.

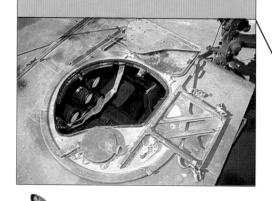

GAS TANK

The gas tank in the rear can hold almost 100 liters of diesel.

DRIVER COMFORT

The seats in this off-road vehicle are very comfortable, and the controls are conveniently placed for the driver. The vehicle's radio is located between the driver and his assistant.

MOBILITY PUT TO THE TEST

The large tires and the independent suspension of this vehicle give it an exceptional capacity for movement and traction over all types of terrain.

EQUIPMENT FOR DRIVING IN WATER

The HUMMER used by the Spanish Marines includes equipment that allows it to drive in the water along the beach. For this purpose, there is a special raised inlet tube on the right side of the engine.

PROPULSION APPARATUS

The latest version of this vehicle incorporates a V8 diesel engine with a cubic capacity of 6,500 cm and 160 hp at 3,400 r.p.m.; there is also a large tilted radiator for cooling the engine.

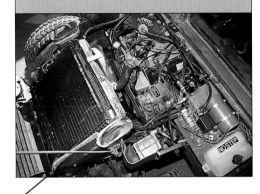

FRONT END

A large sturdy bumper —with two tow rings— protects the capstan, the two large headlights and the front section of the engine from any damage in case of a frontal impact.

TECHNICAL CHARACTERISTICS OF THE HUMMER M998A2

COST IN DOLLARS:	50,000,000
DIMENSIONS:	
Length	187.15 in
Height	72.10 in
Width	71.71 in
Ground clearance	15.37 in
WEIGHT:	
Empty	5,328 lbs
Maximum	7,702 lbs
Maximum cargo	2,375 lbs
Cargo in tow	3,400 lbs
Gas tank capacity	94 l

PROPULSION:	
6.5 liter V8 diesel engine producing 160 hp at 3,400 rpm	
PERFORMANCE:	
Longitudinal gradient	60 %
Transversal gradient	40 %
Depth of crossed body of water	30 inches without equipment, and 60 with it
Maximum speed	70 mph
Turn radius	25 feet
Range	300 miles

The need to transport troops over all types of terrain as quickly as possible has led to the development of a wide range of light vehicles designed to be highly mobile in specific areas, from arid deserts to wet zones.

These means of transport have very specific features, developed according to the needs of their users or based on the producer's personal design. A wide variety of options may be found on the market; some of them are described below.

Lightweight methods for deep penetrations

Vehicles are being produced to improve their capacity for relocating men, and some special elements are being designed to improve their ability to carry out secret missions and detailed reconnaissance; some of these have been derived from existing models.

Proposals for a variety of requirements

Based on the design of the engine and chassis in the Peugeot VLTT P4, engineers from the French company Panhard and Levassor have developed the VEHA (Véhicule Aeromobile), a vehicle that is only 134 inches

"REBECO" OFF-ROAD VEHICLE
The "Rebeco" off road vehicle has gone through an exhaustive series of tests by the Spanish Ministry of Defense to gain the necessary approvals within the category of highly mobile vehicles.

THE SPANISH HUMMER
The Spanish company URO has designed a highly mobile off-road vehicle that, at first glance, looks similar to the HUMMER in terms of its large size. According to its manufacturers, its performance is superior to that of the U.S. model.

in length and can carry cargo weighing a ton. A seat may be installed in the rear from which a third crew member can maneuver various types of weapons. It only weighs 4,190 pounds, so it is easily transported by air. It has a range of 435 miles and can substitute or complement the mechanical mules now in service, including the LOHR Fardier FL500 and FL501 used in France and by the Spanish Paratroopers (BRIPAC) and Legionaries (BRILEG).

Other highly mobile French models are the VLA and VLB, manufactured by LOHR in their Strasbourg factory. The first is a small 4x4 weighing 1.2 t that can transport a patrol of five men and also be used as a lightweight weapons pad. Up to 10 of them may be transported in the cargo hold of a medium-sized transport plane. The latter has a more advanced design with armor-plated elements that increase its weight to 4,850 lbs.

There are also many other light models such as the M-240 Storm produced in Israel by Automotive Industries Limited, transformed to obtain more operational possibilities. The Isrealis have used their experience in combat to produce the M-462 Abir, powered by a 6.5 l diesel engine, which can carry cargo weighing 3,970 lbs or a group of up to 13 men including the driver.

Fast attack and exploration vehicles

Initially designed as a transformation of

the buggies used by civilians on the beach or in the desert, these vehicles, known as FAV (Fast Attack Vehicles), are used by a range of troops including the commandos in the Portugese Army and the U.S Navy SEALs (who used them for a variety of missions during Operation Desert Storm).

During this conflict, the British Special Air Service (SAS) used vehicles called LSV (Light Strike Vehicles). Many other models are still in production; these include the Scorpion made by the U.S. Chenowth Corporation, the Saker made in Britain by Wessex, the Hungarian Szöcske and the Brazilian VAR. Added to the list are some more advanced models such as the VRI (Véhicule Rapide d'Investigation), –developed jointly by Panhard and Chenowth— which combines a range of 560 miles with a capacity to transport a driver, gunner and team leader at a maximum speed of 80 mph. It only weighs 2.6 tons thanks to a superior tubular structure and the use of advanced and compound materials.

At present, various models of the FLYER are also under construction; it is produced by

FRENCH MODEL

The Auverland company proposes their own design for a high mobility light vehicle, developed to fulfill those requirements that demand little weight and a great capacity for movement over the most difficult terrain.

the U.S. company of the same name and has a tubular structure that allows it to carry up to its own weight (2735 lbs) in cargo.

Another important model is the Desert Raider, from Automotive Industries, which has a six-wheel-drive configuration and can transport a crew of three men in front and up to 2,645 lbs of cargo in the back; its design is unique among its kind.

MECHANICAL MULES

During combat missions where it is necessary to move large-sized, light cargo, mechanical mules are very useful; for example, these French LOHR are used by French paratroopers during their maneuvers.

Developed to fulfill the needs of the Special and Rapid Deployment Forces, this Israeli model has a trapezoidal suspension with double shock absorbers on its two axles; it has exceptional maneuverability and can drive over all types of surfaces. In addition, it is very small —only 152 inches in height and 73 inches in width.

CARGO TRANSPORT

The transportation of the containers, munitions or logistical elements of weapons systems requires a lot of effort on the part of the soldiers; therefore, troops transported by air can be helped by specific designs such as this, by the Panhard Company, which includes a rear cargo platform.

New tactical advances developed in the shadow of the HUMMER

The development of the U.S. off-road vehicle, the HUMMER, brought with it a revolution with regard to the performance of a new generation of medium tactical vehicles, generally designed to transport small groups of men and lightweight weapons systems.

TECHNICAL CHARACTERISTICS OF THE VAMTAC "REBECO"

COST IN DOLLARS:	30,000,000	**Gas tank capacity**	110 l
DIMENSIONS:		**PROPULSION:**	
Length	190.89 in	Steyr M16-TCA turbodiesel engine with 6 cylinders, 163 hp and a cubic capacity of 3,200 cm	
Height	74.39 in		
Width	86.25 in	**PERFORMANCE:**	
Ground clearance	17.81 in	Longitudinal gradient	+70 %
WEIGHT:		Transversal gradient	+40 %
Running	from 6,615 to 7,715 lbs according to version	Depth of crossed body of water	30 inches without equipment, and 60 with it
Maximum	11,025 lbs	Maximum speed	80 mph
Maximum cargo	4,410 lbs	Turn radius	25 feet
Cargo in tow	8,820 lbs	Range	375 miles

VAMTAC, Spanish high mobility vehicle

The Spanish project to develop a high mobility tactical vehicle was begun at the company, URO Vehículos Especiales S.A. (UROVESA), in 1995 in response to the Spanish army's desire to incorporate a very maneuverable, off-road vehicle capable of moving 1.5 tons of cargo in all types of trucks. The company's experience in producing medium trucks helped in the development of this model, and 80 % of its components are Spanish. Testing for necessary uniformity began in 1998.

Several configurations have been evaluated pending its arrival which, thanks to its modular design, include a personnel carrier, a general cargo carrier, and one for the transportation of specialized shelters or various

LIGHT ATTACK VEHICLE

The commando patrol's need to cover a lot of ground and respond with heavy fire if discovered infiltrating enemy territory has led to the development of attack vehicles like this one by Panhard.

SPANISH LIGHT TRACTOR VEHICLES

The paratrooper and legionary units of the Spanish army use the FOX-15/D mechanical mules produced by the division of advanced projects and services; these include a front tractor unit and a rear cargo tow bed for moving large loads of men and materials.

weapons systems such as medium machine guns, anti-tank and anti-air missile launchers, and automatic grenade launchers. Capable of operating in temperatures from -4° F – 122° F, the "Rebeco", as it is known in military circles, is mounted on a robust chassis, which is the base for the rest of its elements. Among them is a powerful engine with independent suspension mounted on four large wheels, whose tire pressure can be controlled by the driver.

In addition, it can reach 44.6 hp if empty and 32.6 hp with cargo, which allows for rapid transportation of personnel and 2,205 lbs of all types of equipment. The hooks on the side are used to transport it in the sling of a medium or heavy helicopter, or it can be launched from the air with parachutes and a special landing platform on the ground.

The designs of other countries

Following in the footsteps of the HUMMER, the Japanese firm Kohkidohsha has designed a HMV (High Mobility Vehicle) 4x4 in response to an order in 1992 for almost one hundred units by Japanese defense forces. This vehicle weighs 2.44 tons, measures 193.5 inches and incorporates an automatic gear change box that continuously works off the four wheel motors; it also has doors and a top that can be easily taken apart and is powered by a four cubic liter diesel engine with 150 hp. Its basic configuration can transport four men and up to 3,310 lbs

of cargo, especially all types of parts or standard containers placed in its spacious cargo hold. The VAT, produced by the Italian company, Aplicazione Rielaboraziono Impianti Speciali (ARIS), in its factory in Lombardore, is very similar to this last model. This multipurpose vehicle includes a robust chassis with two crossbeams, which give it a lot of flexibility and many possibilities for torsion. All of this is very useful in achieving the agility necessary to move over all types of terrain.

COMBAT BUGGY

The French company, Doucet, proposes this transformation of a California buggy for use on beaches. It is remarkably mobile and works well in those situations where enemy fire is not expected.

The peculiarities of the Swedish mountainous terrain and the defense policies they have maintained for many years have led to a very high level of technology and industry. Among the leading companies in this country is the automotive firm Scania, whose headquarters is in Södertälje. It manufactures a wide range of civilian and military trucks with engines of various powers, which may be used on land or to power medium-sized vessels; these vehicles have an excellent reputation within the industry worldwide.

Production widely distributed throughout the world

The capacity and performance of the range of Scania engines, designed for military use with a horsepower ranging from 220 to 530, has had an influence on the fact that they've been chosen to power so many vehicles produced in the country and abroad. Among those manufactured abroad are the Mowag Piranha III, Hägglunds CV 90 IFV, Giat Industries Vextra and the BMR/VEC (currently being modernized by the Spanish company Santa Barbara).

ENGINES WIDELY DISTRIBUTED

Many vehicle engines in various countries, including BMR Spanish wheeled armored vehicles, are powered by Scania engines. These include a variety of diesels that range from 9 cubic liters and 220 horsepower to 14 liters and 530 hp.

THE HEAVIEST CARGO

The Scania gondola car 143EK 6x6z has a 450 hp engine in its front cabin, which is powerful enough to move the tractor unit, the gondola and a medium combat tank. All this can weigh up to 100 tons.

Leaders as well in aspects such as operational dependence, operational economics and engineering development, Scania's range includes trucks developed for civilian use and others modified to fulfill the strict requirements of military users; Scania has been producing military vehicles since the 1970's, when they were associated with Vabis.

Priority: transporting all types of cargo

This concept, which governs all the

designs and products of this Swedish company, has led to the configuration of a range of medium, heavy and very heavy vehicles. These vehicles have a common design that combines a chassis with two highly resistant crossbeams, remarkable sturdiness and great flexibility, and a basic configuration to transport cargo up to 100 tons over many types of irregular terrain.

Currently, the trucks can incorporate an optional system, which controls the air suspension via an electronic system called ELC (Electronic Level Control); this system can, for example, vary its rigidity in relation to the cargo or terrain, or it can modify the height of the cargo hold to adapt to the height of the loading bay. Another carefully constructed aspect is the driving cab, made of steel to be able to resist direct impacts of up to a ton. It has a large windshield that allows for great visibility in all directions, and an airbag to protect the driver in case of a frontal collision. It also has a VPS (Vehicle Protection System) that can be used to repel assaults from the exterior or monitor the opening of doors without authorization, and it can incorporate an advanced alarm system that emits waves in varying tones and frequencies so that the driver stays concentrated on his task.

A functional modular design

The Scania range includes classes C, D, G and L, which are designed for specific types of

TRACTOR TOW TRUCK
The Scania 6x4 tractor unit corresponds to model T144GB; known for its capacity to tow 80 tons of cargo on asphalt roads or prepared paths. It has a DSC 14 diesel engine with 530 hp.

HEAVY LOGISTICAL VEHICLE
This 6x6 Scania truck has an axle and two additional tires for those jobs that require more mobility. A large crane has been installed in its cargo hold, which is stabilized by four hydraulic jacks located in each corner of the rear platform.

transport. The first is ideal for construction jobs under difficult conditions; the second is a sturdy alternative for short distances and good roads; the third adapts to a wide range of requirements and necessities; and the fourth is ideal for driving at high speeds with heavy cargo on good roads.

These vehicles benefit from a common technology applied to several significant areas. For example, the G can combine 7 small cabs with other larger ones with a capacity of transporting more passengers. The range of engines is efficient and includes the EDC system, which increases performance as it reduces gas emissions. The gearbox is made by Scania and is offered in various configurations; this includes the Opticruise automatic system with flat ground and gradient options; therefore, the gearbox chooses the adequate gear for each moment, and the driver can concentrate on the road.

Military range for all tactical necessities

The developments of these Swedish trucks have led to the configuration of a wide range of models that fulfill the necessities of tactical transport on the road or over rugged terrain; these vehicles are known for their performance, operational possibilities and cargo capacity when driving on irregular terrain. These aspects have led to the sale of various lots to other countries such as Angola, Brazil (which produces them with a permit), Finland, Greece and Norway.

4 x 4 and 6 x 6 configurations

This range, basically designed to transport various types of cargo, standardized containers or lightweight weapons systems, includes the P93MK4x4Z model, a medium truck with a capacity for unrestricted movement over all types of terrain. It has a front cab with a hatch on the top to hold defense machine guns, and a rear cargo hold covered by a green canvas covering to protect the cargo from inclement weather. It has a length of 281.71 inches and is powered by a DS9 diesel engine with 252 hp that can transport cargo up to 5 t.

The P113HK6x6Z is a truck with three axles that is 350.66 inches in length and is designed to transport standardized containers; it incorporates an automatic Finnish Hooklift HL26.52A system to lift and unload them. It has a cargo capacity of 14 t and a DSC11 engine with 320 hp that works together with the GT800 gearbox.

Even more capable than this last model is the P124CB4x4HZ, which has a similar configuration, measures 265.55 inches, is powered by a DSC1202 engine with 360 hp, and can transport cargo weighing between 6 and 8 t, depending on the terrain. Its cab is an advanced CP14, and its cargo hold is made of steel with aluminum panels. A derivation of the former, but 6 x 6, is the P124CB6x6HZ with the same cab and an "ampiroll" platform in its cargo hold to carry containers or various types of cargo —such as medium caterpillar tracks— as long as their weight does not exceed 19 t. It has a length of 356.18 inches and a DSC12 engine with 360 hp that works together with a GR900 gearbox.

TOTAL MOBILITY

Gradients, sharp curves and ditches are some of the obstacles that Scania four-wheel-drive trucks can easily overcome thanks to their design, their powerful engines, and the quality of their parts.

The P124GB6x2NZ belongs to the same series and has forward-wheel-drive, designed to work on asphalt and roads in good condition. Its comes in various configurations including road sweepers to clean the runways at air bases, dump trucks for cargo, and models for the transportation of containers or cisterns with incorporated pressure. It has a DS12 engine, a length of 350.66 inches and a maximum capacity of 14 t.

TECHNICAL CHARACTERISTICS OF THE P93MK4X4Z SCANIA TRUCK

COST IN DOLLARS:	Unknown	**Maximum cargo**	5 tons
DIMENSIONS:		**Cargo in tow**	20 tons
Length	281.71 in	**PROPULSION:**	
Height	130.02 in	DS9 turbodiesel engine with 252 hp	
Width	97.71 in	**PERFORMANCE:**	
Distance between axles	158 in	Longitudinal gradient	60 %
Ground clearance	22.06 in	Transversal gradient	40 %
WEIGHT:		Depth of crossed body of water	31.52 in
Empty	9 tons	Maximum speed	56 mph
Maximum	14.3 tons	Range	435 miles

A 310 horsepower engine allows for a maximum speed of 56 mph in this Scania P113 HK 8x6, which can transport cargo weighing 20 tons on highways or roads by adapting its special wheel assembly.

Models for special and very heavy cargo

The P113HK8x6/4Z truck has an original configuration with four axles, the front and two rear ones are fitted with wheels with 315/80R2.5 times and the intermediate one has two 285/60R22.5 support tires to give the vehicle more stability. The 3506.6 inch platform is made up of a front cab and a cargo hold that can carry up to 20.5 tons; its DS11 engine works off a GR900R gearbox.

The P124Cb8x6/4HZ has the same configuration of axles. It has a length of 366 inches and can transport the same cargo weight as the last model. Its engine is type DSC12, powerful enough to transport armored caterpillar tracks in the M113 family, which are easily placed on its rear platform (which includes an automatic cargo system). The operational requirements for transporting medium and heavy vehicles necessitates the use of the R143EK6x6Z tractor truck, designed to tow various models of gondola cars with six or more axles, which carry the transported objects. Its cargo capacity is 60 tons, and it has a DSC14 engine with 450 hp;

USED BY THE MILITARY

This 113HK 6x6 Scania truck is one of the vehicles used by the Swedish military to transport shelters associated with logistical system weapons command centers. It can drive over very difficult terrain.

the cab in this truck has front seats for the driver and his assistant, and a rear compartment with its own doors to transport the crew of what is normally a tank weighing fifty tons.

Its general configuration includes some civilian features that have been optimized to function in the inflexible, harsh environments

associated with military tasks. For this reason, it has additional bright headlights on the top to signal its movements and a large cargo capacity, giving it an exceptional range even when it is transporting heavy cargo on the flat bed; these flat beds have twenty-four wheels.

The T144GB6x4NZ is bigger and more powerful than the last. It is 323 inches in length, weighs 13.5 tons, and has a CT19 cabin with room for the DSC14 engine with 530 hp that works off a GRSH900R gearbox. Large 315/80R22.5 tires have been fitted on its wheels, which are ideal for driving on highways and various types of roads, but should not be used on rugged terrain where their movements would be very limited.

This vehicle can transport various gondola cars or mobile platforms up to 120 tons; this makes it ideal for carrying second and third generation heavy combat tanks, including the German Leopard II used by the Swedish Armed Forces.

ARTILLERY EQUIPMENT

URO light trucks can transport light artillery parts and reserves of grenades and explosives at the same time they tow the weapon, which could be an Oto-Melara M56 105 millimeter mortar.

The growth of Spanish industrial capacity during the 1970's brought with it a process of technological consolidation in the area of medium and heavy military vehicles. Until then, this area had been occupied by the great quantity and variety of U.S. vehicles received during the 1950's as a result of agreements signed with U.S. companies.

Since then, several Spanish firms have headed up the production of military trucks designed to fulfill growing national demands and orders from abroad. Thus, the sector has been consolidated so that it is competitive and remarkably self-sufficient.

Small trucks to assist in jobs

Military troops, especially those in the infantry, require a multitude of vehicles to transport the various tactical and logistical systems used in combat. This means the transport of small shelters with communications equipment, medium-weight equipment, or small groups of men —tasks that are ideal for two ton trucks.

BUILT-IN LOGISTICAL TRANSPORT

The installation of the Damrol system in a Pegaso truck allows for the configuration of the 380E3/H Vempar model. It has a tractor unit that can transport 12 tons of cargo and a towed flat bed that can carry up to 20 tons.

Chassis adapted for multiple variants

The introduction of model 1300 light trucks manufactured by Land Rover Santana in its Linares factory did not make a great impression on the Spanish Armed Forces, and the company soon saw the necessity of developing a more advanced model, called the Santana S-2000 Militar. It has four-wheel-drive and is configured with a flat-walled cab at the front, which is capable of holding the dri-

ver and his assistant and houses the engine. Two thirds of the rear is occupied by the cargo hold, which can carry 12 men or material weighing up to 2 tons.

The variants which are also used in other countries, include a mobile command post with a rear structure made of durable aluminum to protect those working inside from inclement weather, and communications models similar to the last, equiped with various radios. There is also a mobile workshop (with a small crane and generator) to repair minor breakdowns during maneuvers, and a logistical cistern with a rear tank for a capacity of 1,600 liters of fuel or water. These models can transport a S-250 shelter fixed with slings to the back end and an electrical generator and mobile illumination equipment, which enables specific places, such as centers in the chain of command and logistics, to be illuminated.

A timber truck arrives on the scene

The Spanish URO Special Vehicles company, in Santiago de Compostela, designed and produced light trucks adapted to narrow forest roads when four of its products underwent

DISTRIBUTED TO THE ARMY

The Spanish Army has more than ten thousand Pegaso trucks in various types and models. Among them is the 3046 model four-wheel-drive model, which is used to transport medium cargo like these containers for electronic war equipment.

various tests for potential adoption by the military. In 1984, the army decided to incorporate the first units of URO model U-12.13 after it had been approved by the Ministry of Defense for the period 1984-1989. In 1990 it was model MT-149 AT, and since 1997 it has been the MAT-18.16.13SE. The military range of the company includes 9 different models, which use engines from 143 to 230 horsepower and have a maximum authorized weight of between 17,650 and 30,875 pounds.

GONDOLA CAR UNIT

Pegaso has produced various 7345 tractor units for the Spanish Army and Navy. They are a variant of civilian trucks, which can transport the flat beds that carry armored vehicles and tanks on the highway.

Its cargo capacity is 2 tons on any type of terrain. It is also highly maneuverable: it can turn in a space of only 23 feet and pass over 100 % longitudinal gradients and 40 % transversals. Its chassis is very flexible, for good roadholding, and it is easy to maintain —because its various components are easily accessible. There are many possibilities for a wide variety of configurations. These include minibuses with 16 places, transport trucks for general cargo, launch pads for anti-air canons, communications vans, ambulances with four stretchers, mobile workshops, cisterns, water tanks, platforms with cranes, fire trucks, snowplows, etc., always depending on the necessities of the user.

These qualities and the fact that all the versions are easy to produce has led to its export to Algeria, Argentina, Belgium, Brazil, Chile, Egypt, Saint Thomas, Morocco, Mozambique, Tunisia and Uruguay. In addition, it has been used at the headquarters of the European army since 1997. These orders bring annual production to about 250 units.

Heavy trucks, various configurations and producers

The use of the technology of the Dutch firm DAF helped the Spanish Empresa Nacional de Autocamiones S.A. (ENASA) to get their Pegaso 3045 model officially approved for the period 1970-1975. Several thousand of these models were manufactured and exported to Burkina Faso, Chile and Nicaragua.

> **TRACTOR CAB**
>
> Kynos produces a tractor cab with four axles and eight motored wheels that can transport cargo up to sixty tons over all types of terrain. This model is versatile and has an excellent range.

The Pegaso 4 x 4 and 6 x 6

The 3045D model was a 4x4 truck with a Pegaso 9026/13 diesel engine with 125 hp that could transport cargo of 3 tons over difficult terrain or up to 6 tons on the road. As production of this model continued, the need for more capable models arose. This led to the production of the Pegaso 3046/50 with the same capacity as the 3045D, the 3046/10 which can hold up to 5 tons and is four-wheel-drive, the 7217/16 with a 170 hp engine and the 7222A with a 220 hp engine and a longer chassis. Egypt ordered 2,650 units in 1980 and another 9,000 in 1981. However, not all of these orders were delivered due to payment problems. Other countries that have bought it are Morocco, Peru, Somalia and Nigeria (which ordered some of the 4 tons, 3040 models).

The development of the truck with two axles brought with it the production of a larger 6x6 model called the Pegaso 3050. With a cargo capacity of 6 tons on difficult terrain and 10 tons on the road, this chassis has been used in the configuration of a large family of logistical trucks, mobile cranes, tire drillers, launchers of Teruel rockets, etc. In 1982, a new model was developed with a

redesigned cab for more comfortable driving and a Pegaso engine with an improved power of 220 hp.

In 1987, this last model was replaced with the 7327 model, with a 225 hp engine. More than a thousand units were exported to Morocco, and various subvariants from A1 to A6 have been produced.

Tactical mobility and logistics of massive cargo

During the 1970's, production began on the first units of the Talbot Barreiros R-3464 tractor cab 6x4, and since 1987, the 6x6 Pegaso 7345; both were designed to tow flat beds for cars and especially heavy materials (weighing up to 165,375 lbs in the case of the 6x6 Pegaso 7345). Other complementary models were introduced that, since 1988, have included the Aljaba tractor cab, manufactured by the Kynos S.A. factory, with an 8x8 configuration and a 525 hp engine. It can transport cargo up to seventy tons over any type of terrain, and it has a range of 620 miles. This powerful truck has been acquired by the Spanish Army and Navy and has been exported to South Africa, where it is produced with a permit under the name "Cavallo".

Currently, with the aim of strengthening

THE URO MAT-18.16

The URO MAT-18.16 was introduced in the showroom of Eurosatory in 1998. It is a tactical off-road vehicle that can transport a total of 26,450 lbs; it also has a 180 hp engine that can overcome the most difficult obstacles.

their connection to the logistical truck market, Pegaso is producing the 380E3/H Vempar special vehicle, a 6x4 vehicle with a flat bed in tow. Its technical variant is a 6x6 vehicle of 10 tons known as the 250.37W. Both models have a Damrol system to hoist the cargo automatically. The tractor unit has a cab for two men and a 310 hp diesel engine and can hold 12 tons of cargo in the truck and another 20 tons on the flat bed.

EXPORT ORDERS

Morocco is one of that various users of Spanish Pegaso trucks; it has made various orders in the last two decades for a total of several thousand units. Among these is the 3055, configured with a cistern to transport fuel, and painted a desert color.

FRONT GRILLE

The front bumper includes the headlights and the war light for driving at night, a towline and a tow hook. The upper part has a series of bars to protect the front grille from minor impacts.

LARGE SIDE MIRRORS

The elevated position of the driver and the inability to see the central rear area requires the use of large side mirrors to help the driver maneuver more carefully.

ENGINE UNDER THE CAB

The Pegaso 9100/42 six cylinder diesel engine with 170 hp is located between the cab floor and the front axle. It is powerful enough to move this two-axle truck over any type of terrain, even when it is carrying cargo.

TECHNICAL CHARACTERISTICS OF THE PEGASO 4X4 7217A TRUCK

COST IN DOLLARS:	83,400,000	Gas tank capacity	350 l
DIMENSIONS:		**PROPULSION:**	
Length	277.77 in	Pegaso model 9100/42 diesel engine with 6 cylinders and 170 hp at 2,100 r.p.m.	
Height	108.55 in		
Width	94.8 in	**PERFORMANCE:**	
Ground clearance	12.6 in	Longitudinal gradient	70 %
WEIGHT:		Transversal gradient	30 %
Empty	1,485 lbs	Depth of crossed body of water	40 in
Maximum	27,000 lbs	Maximum speed	56 mph
Maximum cargo	11,025 lbs	Turn radius	37 feet
Cargo in tow	16,535 lbs	Range	560 miles

METAL FRAMEWORKS FOR THE CANVAS

The metal frameworks that allow for a canvas covering over the cargo hold to protect it from inclement weather are usually located at the front end of the cargo hold.

COLLAPSIBLE WALLS

The walls that form the cargo hold can be dismantled for those loading and unloading missions that require a lot of space.

CARGO HOLD

With two benches at the sides to transport up to twenty soldiers, the cargo hold is large and has supports for the metal frameworks that hold up the canvas covering, which protects the compartment.

DRIVER'S SEAT

The driver's seat in Pegaso trucks is comfortable and has a large steering wheel for easy maneuvering; it also has a spartan seat, designed for military use, and gauges indicating the level of fuel, engine temperature, etc.

TOTAL MOBILITY

Each of the four motored wheels is associated with an axle for complete mobility over any type of terrain. The springs have shock absorbers for irregular terrain, and the noiseless gas exit is located in front of the left rear wheel.

The Italian automotive sector includes several very important companies. The reputation of their products has led to their export all over the world. At the same time, Italy's policy of economic growth has encouraged the purchase of foreign companies, such as the Spanish firm Pegaso, from where they jointly produce vehicles.

In the area of medium and heavy tactical military vehicles, two important companies are Iveco, part of Fiat and located in Bolzano, and Astra, whose headquarters is in Piacenza. Both companies have a wide range of products distributed amongst the Italian Armed Forces and exported in great quantities abroad.

Models designed to maneuver over any type of terrain

Military and security troops require vehicles specially designed and conditioned to endure the harshness of the battlefield where the majority of traveling is done over rugged terrain, and it is unusual to drive on asphalt roads. In addition, they must fulfill other requirements such as the toughness of materials, logistical necessities, low maintenance levels, low infrared emissions and reduced fuel consumption (for increased range); all of this and a superior level of performance..

HIGH MOBILITY

The Iveco M 115.18 WM medium truck has principally been designed to operate on the road, although it has enough power to transport cargo weighing between 4 and 5 tons on forest roads or over snow-covered ground.

LARGE SIZE

Almost 18 tons of equipment and materials can be transported in the cargo hold of the Iveco M 320 E 42 W, a vehicle with four axles and eight motored wheels designed to move over any surface.

Light 4 x 4 truck

These requirements marked the transformation of the Daily commercial van into the Iveco P40 light truck, initially designed to equip troops transported by air. When production was initiated, its name was changed to 40.10 WM.

It has a traditional configuration: a cab for the driver and two assistants, a 2.5 liter turbodiesel engine with 103 hp located in the front, and a cargo hold in the back. The cargo hold can carry 10 men or up to 3,300 pounds of cargo, or it can be configured with various cabs to become an evacuation ambulance, a command post or a mobile workshop.

In addition to its excellent design characteristics (proven in combat during the Italian deployments in Somalia), it can easily move over arid, muddy or snow-covered land, and it can tow 105 millimeter artillery pieces or flat beds up to 1.5 tons. In addition to the Italian army (which has 1,500 units), it has been acquired by the Belgium gendarmerie, Canada (which has manufactured 2,750 units with a permit), the Spanish Army, Holland and Portugal.

Based on the standard vehicle, a variant called the WM/P was developed to transport a structure made of ballistic steel with capacity for six men inside, who are protected by its shield of armor and large observation windows.

Trucks with two axles in several configurations

In recent years, the Italian company Iveco has manufactured various models of 4 x 4 tactical trucks including the 75 PM13 model with a capacity of two tons, the 75.14 WM for

2.5 tons, and the 3.90 PM 16 for 4 tons. The 90.17 WM has been produced in multiple logistical versions, and the 6602 can transport 13,605 lbs. However, ASTRA has manufactured the 4x4 MB-201 for 4 tons, which is widely distributed amongst the Italian Armed Forces and has been exported to Portugal, Singapore and Somalia, among other countries.

Iveco's current proposal is made up of two high-performance models: the M 110.18 WM and the M 115.18 WM. The first has a length of between 252.87 and 264.69 inches and can transport 11,025 or tow 14,110 thanks to its 178 hp engine; it has six gears and a maximum speed of 56 mph. The second model has a rounder driver's cabin and is 7.8 inches longer; it can only go 50 mph as it is a bit higher and wider.

More power and greater mobility

Some phases of combat require the rapid transport of large quantities of logistical elements and the shifting around of big pieces of equipment, a task entrusted to heavy trucks with three or four axles.

MOBILE COMMAND POST

The command post of the Spanish X Bandera Legionaria incorporates various Iveco light 40.10 trucks, which transport shelters for different sections of the general staff. The men work inside, protected from inclement weather.

Cargo capacity superior to 6 tons

This objective led the Italian company Iveco, at the beginning of the 1970's, to develop the 6606 models with six-wheel-drive, designed to tow artillery pieces. A complementary model was designed in 1973 called the 6007 CM; it had three axles and a higher cargo capacity of 10 tons on asphalt roads. The vehicles were used in Italy, Libya and

Somalia. Then other models were developed; the 230.35 WM, which was purchased by Abu Dhabi, and the 260.35 WM, with a configuration of 6 x 4 and 6 x 6 and a cargo capacity of 22,050 lbs.

Iveco's current production encompasses two very powerful models. The first is the M 250.37 WM with three axles and six-wheel-drive, capable of moving 12 tons cargo and towing 19 tons.

It has a 370 hp diesel engine and a maximum speed of over 56 mph. The second model is an 8 x 8 and is known as the M 320 E 42 W; it is powered by a 420 hp engine, with which it can transport 17.5 tons of cargo, even on 60 % gradients.

ASTRA does its part by manufacturing 6 x 6 vehicles of the model BM 20, capable of transporting 10 tons over difficult terrain and 15 tons on the road; they have been modified to satisfy the requirements of the Italian Engineer Arm. They are equipped with the variants NC2, configured as a mobile works-

MEDIUM TRUCKS
Iveco's range of medium off-road vehicles includes the M 100.18 WM with two axles and a 5 ton capacity. It has six gears and the size of its tires is 14.5 R 20.

hop, the NP1, with a drill to make 655 foot deep holes in the ground, the NR2 with a 20 tons crane that was developed in 1983, and the NB1, to transport small vessels for crossing rivers. The BM 309F series has also been designed; it is powered by an eight cylinder

AMPHIBIOUS USE
This Iveco light 40.10 is one of the trucks used by the Italian Marines of the San Marco battalion. It is intended to transport personnel and includes a stand for a medium-weight machine gun on the top of the cargo hold.

engine with 253 hp and can transport cargo weighing up to 33 tons.

Tractor truck for the transport of tanks and armored vehicles

The need for the strategic transportation of the Italian Leopard I tank battalions to cut down on the wear and tear they suffer from traveling long distances led to the development of the Iveco 320.45 WTM tractor truck.

With a 6 x 6 configuration and towing a Bartoletti TCS-50 BO gondola car (originally designed by OTO-Melara), this truck can travel up to 600 km on the 500 liters that fit in its gas tank.

POLICE BUS

Iveco's experience in developing a wide range of trucks has aided in the development of other vehicles, such as this armor-plated bus designed to transport police intervention groups to the deployment zone.

TECHNICAL CHARACTERISTICS OF THE IVECO 40.10 WM LIGHT 4 X 4 TRUCK

COST IN DOLLARS:	55,000,000		Gas tank capacity	70 l
DIMENSIONS:			**PROPULSION:**	
Length	183 in		8142 four cylinder turbodiesel engine with 2.5 cubic liters and	
Height	88.26 in		103 hp at 3,780 r.p.m.	
Width	78.8 in		**PERFORMANCE:**	
Ground clearance	10.48 in		Longitudinal gradient	60 %
WEIGHT:			Transversal gradient	30 %
Empty	6,400 lbs		Depth of crossed body of water	27.58 in
Maximum	9,700 lbs		Maximum speed	62 mph
Maximum cargo	3,300 lbs		Turn radius	19.7 feet
Cargo in tow	3,300 lbs		Range	300 miles

SUFFICIENT MOBILITY

The front of the driver's cab houses the turbodiesel engine with 2.5 cubic liters and 130 hp; it can produce a maximum speed of 62 mph.

FRONT GRILLE

This photo shows some interesting details such as the crankcase at the bottom, the headlights that are built into the vehicle and protected by bars, and the various air inlets that cool the engine and circulate air through the driver's cabin.

IDENTIFICATION FOR WAR ZONES

The large red crosses on the sides of this evacuation ambulance identify its mission and should be enough to prevent the enemy from opening fire on it (although that is not always the case).

SIGNAL LIGHTS

The top of this transport cab for the wounded has two orange-colored lights that identify it as a medical vehicle and, depending if they are lit or not, the type of mission it is completing.

MEDICAL UNIT

The Spanish Army uses the Iveco 40.10 light medical evacuation vehicle, which includes a rear cab with two stretchers at the bottom and two more above them and a seat at the back for the attending medical worker.

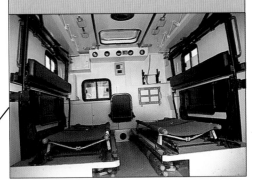

REAR AXLE

This view of one of the two rear wheels on the back axle shows the structure of the fender built into the rear interior, the springs that support the tires over difficult terrain, and the metal rim joined to the axle by six thick nuts and bolts.

DRIVER'S CAB

Iveco 40.10 WM Italian light trucks incorporate a driver's seat that is very similar to that in civilian vehicles. It includes several locks in different places to start the engine, lock the doors, take out the spare tire and open the back compartment.

FUEL TANK

The fuel tank is located under the rear cab against the chassis; it can hold 70 liters of diesel, which gives it a range of about 300 miles.

The necessities for logistical and tactical movements required by the four divisions of the U.S. Armed Forces, the most powerful military in the world, have contributed to the purchase of thousands of trucks designed to fulfill specific, yet varied requirements.

The U.S automobile industry, the world market leader, is made up of a good number of companies specializing in the production of trucks of all sizes. These vehicles have been exported to friendly countries or those receiving military aid.

LARGE VARIETY OF MODELS

Oshkosh manufactures a great variety of heavy trucks, including this 10x10 PLS, which is designed to transport several containers.

MOBILE COMMAND POST

A large shelter has been installed on the cargo platform of this 6x6 truck; it is air-conditioned and has four jacks on the sides to support it on the ground when the vehicle is stopped. It is used as a mobile command post for mechanized units.

Post-war necessities

The end of the Second World War brought with it the storage of enormous amounts of equipment used during the conflict, though by this time most of it worn out due to its constant use in less than ideal conditions.

With this in mind, at the end of the 1940's, the Reo and the Truck and Bus division of General Motors was assigned to produce a new family of tactical trucks; 5,000 units were ordered in 1950.

Development of 6 x 6 trucks with three axles

The outbreak of the Korean War led to the development of several variants that incorporated OA-3321 Reo or COA-331 Continental gasoline engines. The trucks were named after their engines and were produced with 2.5 or 5 tons of cargo capacity. In addition, they manufactured the M35 and M36 for general cargo, the M49, a fuel cistern, the M50, a water tank, the M109 with a shelter for equipment, and the M342, a dump truck, 150,000 of this last model were produced until 1980. About thirty countries have purchased and still use various series of

TECHNICAL CHARACTERISTICS OF THE M1078, 2.5 TON 4 X 4 TRUCK

COST IN DOLLARS:	Varies according to number of units ordered		PROPULSION:		
DIMENSIONS:			Caterpillar 3116 ATAAC 6.6 turbodiesel engine with 6 cylinders and 225 hp at 2,600 r.p.m.		
Length	252.95 in		**PERFORMANCE:**		
Height	125.35 in		Longitudinal gradient	60	%
Width	96.06 in		Transversal gradient	30	%
Ground Clearance	22.02 in		Depth of crossed body of water without equipment	32	in
WEIGHT:			Depth of crossed body of water with equipment	60	in
Empty	15,960 lbs		Maximum speed	58	mph
Maximum cargo	5,000 lbs		Turn radius		
Cargo in tow	12,000 lbs		Range	+400	miles

these models; these countries include Bolivia, Brazil, South Korea, Spain, Honduras, Guatemala, Morocco, Sudan, Turkey and Zaire. At the beginning of the 1990's, the U.S. Army had 65,000 units in use and was working on modernizing several thousand of them as part of the Extended Service Program (ESP).

The M54 is more powerful than these last models; it has been produced since the beginning of the 1950's by Mack and Kaiser Jeep — now known as AM General— in the cargo and tractor variants M51, M52, M54, M55,

TWENTY YEARS OF USE

The U.S trucks from the M939 series have a cargo capacity of five tons and, since they began to be used in 1979, have been proven sturdy. The model in the photograph is a M923 configured for general cargo.

M62 and M64. They can transport cargo up to 10,000 pounds and tow up to 13 tons, in the cargo model, and 24 tons, in the tractor model. These models have been exported to South Korea, Spain and Turkey and have been manufactured with a permit by Italy as the CP56. A new model on the production chain is the M809 series, which includes a NHC-250 diesel engine with 240 hp.

From 1970 to the mid-1980's, a total of 38,000 units, in ten different variants, of the M809 series were produced. They continue to be used, and their sturdiness and cargo

capacity have led to their purchase by Saudi Arabia, China, Jordan, Sudan and Thailand. AM General has also produced the five ton M939 series and sold 22,789 units to the U.S. Army Tank Automotive Command. In 1992, 17,092 more were ordered by the BMY-Wheeled Vehicles Division to fulfill certain internal orders.

A new era of mobility

Stewart and Stevenson Services is a company based in Sealy, Texas that produces a family of medium tactical trucks, and was selected by the U.S. Army in 1991 to manufacture Light Medium Tactical Vehicles (LMTV) of 2.5 tons and Medium Tactical Vehicles (MTV) of 5 tons. These vehicles were designed from the Austrian Steyr 12 M 18, and more than 10,000 have already been delivered.

Designed to last and to be able to complete their mission, these vehicles have been optimized so that the interface between man and machine is as simple as possible. They are configured with a reinforced structure that is resistant to impacts and is highly mobile; they also have components that allow for their easy transport in helicopters or airplanes. In addition, they possess a powerful engine with a flexible chassis, tires to absorb the irregularities of the terrain, an electronically controlled transmission, and a central system to control the tire pressure.

M977 TRUCK

This 8x8 M977 truck, with a capacity to transport 38,800 kilograms, was used in Saudi Arabia for logistical missions during the Persian Gulf War against Iraq in 1991.

TRUCK FOR HEAVY EQUIPMENT

The Oshkosh M1070 is a 8x8 tractor unit that corresponds to HETS (Heavy Equipment Transport Specification) and is designed to transport the heaviest combat tanks, such as the Abrams M1A1.

Both models incorporate a 6-cylinder Caterpillar turbodiesel engine with 225 hp in the light model and 290 hp in the 5 ton one. This is connected to an Allison MD-D7 automatic transmission with 7 gears. The M1080 model with two axles has a standard chassis for a 2.5 ton truck, a length of 252.16 inches, an empty weight of 13,560 lbs and a range of 400 miles. It is available in three versions: one with only a chassis, the M1078 with a cargo hold, and a van with a shelter in the rear. Its older brother has three tractor axles and is offered in 11 different models with short and long chassis and various configurations according to its assigned use. The standard variant is 274.22 inches long, weighs 19,600 lbs and can tow up to 20,400 lbs.

To solve some problems that restricted operations from 1998 to the beginning of 1999, some transformation kits have been designed to recondition the vehicles for further use at their maximum potential.

The largest cargo capacity without restrictions of movement

Certain logistical cargo and the transport of specific weapons systems —ranging from vessels so that the engineers can set up bridges to Patriot anti-air missile launchers— require the use of trucks designed to transport heavy weight without allowing the condition of the terrain to restrict their movements.

Models optimized for military use

A study carried out in 1977 by the U.S. Army Automotive Material Readiness Command (TARCOM) established that trucks originally designed for civilian use could be used in various military tasks; after studying the proposals of six manufacturers, AM General Corporation was chosen to produce 5,507 units of the M915 model at a price of 252.8 million dollars.

These vehicles, based on the Centaur design by the Crane Carrier Company in Tulsa, were delivered over a period of four years and another 2,511 of the M915A1 were produced in 1981. They have a 6x4 configuration and are powered by a Cummins engine with 400 hp, which can tow containers up to 17 tons. Several variants of this model are the M915A2, which entered into service in November 1990, the M916 with a 6x6 configuration, the M917 8x6 with a large dump truck, the M918, which can carry a 56,775 liter tank, and the M919 and M920.

Another U.S. model is the Mack

COMBAT SUPPORT VEHICLE

The mission assigned to this M977 HEMTT (Heavy Expanded Mobility Tactical Truck) by Oshkosh is the transport of these reloading containers for the MLRS multiple rocket launcher to the location of the launch vehicle.

RM6866SX, with a configuration of 6x6 and 22,050 lbs of capacity, which is produced in Pennsylvania and is used to transport cargo or tow artillery pieces. This last model has been purchased by several countries including Australia, which has produced it with a permit as the MC3 since 1983.

Another 1980's model is the Oshkosh MK48 8x8 with an articulated cab and a cargo capacity of up to 50 tons on asphalt roads. Its operational possibilities have led to

VARIED RANGE

The U.S. Army uses a wide range of tactical trucks to support the movements of their large armored and mechanized formations. This group includes more than 100,000 trucks of varying weights.

several orders for 1,482 units by the marines; these orders came in five different configurations called MK48/14 to 18, which varied according to their intended use. Very similar to this last model is the M977 HEMTT (Heavy Expanded Mobility Tactical Truck) series, also by Oshkosh, which has been manufactured for the army since 1981. Units have been exported to Saudi Arabia, Bahrain, South Korea, Egypt and Israel; some have also been delivered to U.S. Customs as support for radar-controlled hot-air balloons used in border surveillance missions.

More than 15,000 units of this truck have been produced, including the M977 cargo transport model, the M978 with a 9500 liter fuel tank, the M983 tractor truck, the M984A1 recovery model and the M985 for transporting MLRS multiple rocket launcher systems. Their common features include an 8 x 8 configuration, a maximum weight of 27 tons and a Detroit Diesel 8V-92TA engine with 445 hp. Based on the HEMTT, Oshkosh designed a 10x10 truck to transport the PLS (Palletized Loan System) with a Multilift MK V cargo system at the front for the automatic loading of the containers; it also tows a M1076 trailer for a total cargo capacity of 30 tons. Since 1992, 2,626 units have been manufactured for tasks ranging from transporting palletized fuel tanks to serving as launch pads for the THAAD system of anti-air missiles.

The Oshkosh Corporation, located in Washington in the town by the same name, is also in charge of the production of 2,000 units of the M911 6x6 tractor module and more than 1,000 units of the advanced M1070 8 x 8; both models have received the designation HET (Heavy Equipment Transporter). The first has been exported to ten different countries, and both are capable of towing gondola cars, which can carry 60 tons of combat tanks over a distance of more than 435 miles.

The French defense industry is the third most important in the world for its productive capacity because of the high demand from its own Armed Forces and police, which follow a policy of purchasing all their equipment from their own industries. French companies have also signed many contracts with countries located in the most remote parts of the world, especially those in the Persian Gulf.

The need to fulfill a variety of criteria has led to the existence of various companies that produce trucks of all sizes such as Acmat, Berliet, Brimont, FFSA, Lohr and Renault. They offer a wide range of products, most of which have been proven in combat by the French or their clients.

Renault, a first rate automobile company

Well known throughout the world for the quality and performance of the vehicles and vans it produces for the civilian market, this French firm, which had its 100th anniversary in 1998, started producing military elements after the First World War. Years of experience in manufacturing small and large series of vehicles, such as the more than five thousand VAB armored vehicles, and the development of a sustained and varied range of products has made them a leader in the field.

COMPLETE PROTECTION

Renault offers several armored cabs for its range of TRM 1000, KERAX and GBC 180 trucks; these trucks can block impacts of 7.62 mm caliber from 330 feet away.

UPDATED PERFORMANCE

Renault has reconditioned 4,500 units of the 4 ton Berliet GBC 8 truck, which is now known as the GBC 180 and includes a new engine with 175 hp, increasing its radius of action and maximum speed.

Wide range introduced in France and other countries

Renault has produced various models of light trucks such as: the B110 Turbo 4 x 4, with a cargo capacity of between 1,600 and 3,800 pounds depending if the 35D or the 45D chassis is used, the TRM 1200 4x4 with a 4-cylinder Renault 712 diesel engine with 72 hp, almost four thousand of which have been exported to Algeria and Morocco, and the TRM 2000 4 x 4 for 2 tons of cargo, which is produced in the standard variant and a high mobility model with a higher ground clearance. Since production began in 1981, 12,000 units have been purchased by the French Army, 190 by Morocco, 50 by Namibia, 10 by Qatar and 85 by the FINUL.

The range of medium trucks includes the TRM 4000 4 x 4 designed in 1973; it is based on the Saviem SM8 commercial vehicle and can transport 4-5 tons of cargo. 7,500 of them have been produced with a 133 hp engine for the French Army and an indefinite number have been exported to various countries.

Another 4x4 series is configured by the models TRM 160, TRM 180, TRM 200 and TRM 230, of which at least seven optimized variants have been produced to transport between 5 and 8 tons. They are powered

with engines of between 159 and 226 hp and are equipped with 275 liter gas tanks, which give them a range of close to 625 miles

Some of the heaviest trucks are the TRM 9000 6x6, which can carry up to 9 tons and tow 10 tons; 500 have been exported to Algeria, 38 to Saudi Arabia, 50 to Egypt and 1,500 to Morocco. Two other heavy models are the TRM 1000 6 x 6, which was developed in 1985 and can transport large containers or various systems such as the Tropomil radar, and the TRM 340.34 6 x 6, which has a 335 hp engine and can carry up to 36,200 lbs. This last model has been modified as a tractor truck capable of towing semi-trailers with a total cargo of up to 143,325 lbs. The company has also introduced the R 390 6 x 4 tractor cab, designed to transport on the road combat tanks weighing up to 55 tons on a Nicolas STA 43 gondola car.

Their proposal for the future

In addition to production of these models, which are constantly being tested to update their components, Renault also currently offers various solutions for the future. This includes the TRM 10000 Valorisé with an automatic loading and unloading system for

ACQUIRED BY BELGIUM

The Renault 385.40 8x4 truck was designed in 1996 as a mobile logistical unit with a high performance capacity. 27 units have already been exported to Belgium.

HEAVY TRACTOR TRUCK

The Renault TRM 700-100 is a 6x6 tractor truck that can tow up to 90 tons; it can easily transport combat tanks such as the third generation Leclerc.

an increase in cargo capacity of 2 tons, a mobility kit to change the tire pressure from the driver's cabin, an ABS kit to improve the brakes, and an armor-plated cabin to protect its occupants from light artillery fire.

Armor plating can also be used on the Berliet GBC 6 x 6 thanks to the design of the GBC 180 cab, which can incorporate an anti-mine layer on the bottom and a system of protection against nuclear, chemical and biological threats. A total of 4,500 units of this model are being modernized as a result of the Direction

Générale de l'Armement program, which includes changes in the engine, the cab, the electrical elements, the steering and the brakes.

Other models in production are the Kerax 8 x 8 truck for logistical tasks, 27 of which have been purchased by the Belgian Armed Forces since 1998, the TRM 200.13 6 x 6 which can transport 4-8 tons of cargo and is a result of the militarization of the civilian range of vehicle, and the TRM 700-100 tank carrier with a 700 hp engine to transport battalions of Leclerc tanks.

Other French companies which produce military trucks

Other minor companies (although not in term of productive power) have sprung up in Renault's shadow. They concentrate on the production of other types of vehicles and the creation of smaller specialized series that fulfill specific requirements, which, in some cases, are considerably different from the performance of vehicles in mass production.

ACMAT, the Atlantic's machine builder

From their factories in Saint-Nazaire, they produce various models of trucks used by the French Armed Forces and 35 other countries, including Burkina Faso, Cameroon, Chad, the Ivory Coast, Gabon, Gambia, Ireland, Morocco, Senegal, Somalia and Zambia.

MAXIMUM TORSION
This photo shows the torsion of the crossbeams of the chassis on this Renault truck as it drives over rocky terrain. This requires special design and production features.

LOGISTICAL AND ARMOR-PLATED
This Renault TRM 10000 6x6 truck with 10 tons of cargo capacity has been modified to transport containers. It loads automatically and has an armor-plated cab to protect the crew.

Their current range is made up of VLRA, a liaison, reconnaissance and support vehicle, which comes in a 4 x 4 tactical van and a 6 x 6 truck. The first model is the TPK series, with a family of 32 variants designed for various necessities ranging from transporting multiple rocket launchers to specific models acquired by the French commandos for completing missions quickly. Their radius of action is more than 1,000 miles, and they have a cargo capacity of between 15 and 21 people or 1.5 to 3.5 tons of cargo. The second model is produced in 21 variants, which can cross 35.45 inch rivers and transport a large number of weapons and logistical systems, including the shelters for the Roland anti-air missile system. It can carry 3.5 to 6.5 tons of cargo or tow up to 6 tons.

Since the end of the 1980's, the VLRA 8 x 8 has been produced, a 6 tons logistical truck with a high capacity for movement due to its special configuration of four axles divided into two and two. This particular feature has led to its acquisition by the French and the Moroccans as an element to be transported by air.

These last models are joined by the VLA front lines logistical vehicle, produced in 8 variants with 4 x 4, 6 x 6 and 8 x 8 configurations. A majority of these variants were deployed in the Gulf War, where they had a low level of required maintenance and some good logistical capacities. The model with two axles is called the WPK 4.40 STL and includes a Perkins 180 hp diesel engine, a cargo capacity of 11,025 lbs and a range of 808 miles, thanks to its 420 liter gas tank. The three axle model is known as the WPK 6.66 STL and can transport 8 tons over a dis-

LOGISTICAL NECESSITIES
The French Army's many transport necessities require the use of a wide range of vehicles adapted for different cargo capacities and activities. One example is the Renault TRM 4000 and 9000.

RENAULT TRM 200.13 TRUCKS
Renault TRM 200.13 trucks are the militarization of a civilian range. They are designed to move weights of between 4 and 8 tons, and 90% of their components are the same as those trucks mass produced for civilian use.

tance of 620 miles. The WPK 8.70 STL has four axles, a 210 hp turbodiesel engine, and can carry 10 tons in its multipurpose cargo hold, which can also transform into a platform.

Production of more specialized models

Founded in 1963 to produce industrial vehicles, Lohr started producing military equipment ten years later in its Strasbourg factory. It currently divides its industrial efforts into three parts: SRBP semi flat bed trucks which, together with the Scania SMC 60 6 x 3 DB truck, have been purchased by the Belgians, the Caesar artillery system, which consists of a 6 x 6 truck to transport a 155/45 mm system and its operators, and the WLP 14 logistical system, which is used by the German Army.

Currently, they are working on several models of 6 x 6 trucks equipped with shelters and a centerpole so that the radar antenna may be placed up high to increase its surveillance range. They are also reconditioning the Roland cabs under the Carol/Carola program, replacing them with lighter models made of aluminum. In addition, they produce other trucks modified with the MATS/DEP-

TECHNICAL CHARACTERISTICS OF THE RENAULT TRM 160.11 TRUCK

COST IN DOLLARS:	Unknown	**Cargo in tow**	13,230 lbs
DIMENSIONS:		**Gas tank capacity**	275 l
Length	269.5 in	**PROPULSION:**	
Height	113.87 in	MIDS 06-02-26W diesel engine with 159 hp at 2,600 r.p.m.	
Width	91.49 in	**PERFORMANCE:**	
Ground Clearance	12.81 in	Longitudinal gradient	50 %
WEIGHT:		Transversal gradient	30 %
Empty	11,245 lbs	Angles of approximation/departure	30° / 40°
Maximum	25,350 lbs	Maximum speed	58 mph
Maximum cargo	11,900 lbs	Range	620 miles

96 system, which consists of pre-loaded panels made of octagonal elements. These can be used to set up a path to facilitate the circulation of launch vehicles for Exocet MM40 missiles, which are designed to defend the coast from mobile batteries. The vehicles are equipped with a palletized cargo system or a PLM 17 arm, which quickly hoists and positions the containers, or are configured to launch and collect the modules of the Leguan tactical bridge.

COMBAT TRUCK

The commandos of the French Army have purchased this Acmat light-weight 4x4 truck for deep combat missions; its cargo hold has a half a dozen stands for all types of machine guns and support weapons to help with missions against enemy forces.

After the break-up of the two countries, the Czech Republic was left with a majority of the productive potential. This included the automotive company, Tatra, which specialized in the manufacture of trucks of varying sizes, superior in terms of operational potential, sturdiness and low purchase price.

Range adapted to a variety of necessities

Tatra has changed a lot since it first began work in 1908. This is a result of the continued experience of producing designs such as the T 29 with three axles, which was developed to tow artillery pieces, the T 111 manufactured at the beginning of the 1940's, the famous T 138 used by the Czechoslovakian Army during the 1960's, and the reputable T 813, which was even exported to India.

This exper-ience in designing new models has led to the continued development of more advanced trucks in terms of their configurations for general use or modifications for specific requirements. They are different from other companies' models because they include a very flexible chassis, which adapts well to the terrain and absorbs any irregularities. All these qualities and its good reputation mean that several groups of the T 815 model have been chosen to participate in UN peacekeeping missions.

A chassis that allows for the configuration of requested models

Since the end of the 1980's, the T 815 series has replaced units of the T 813 model; the 6 x 6 and 8 x 8 versions were manufactured first and then the 4 x 4. The latter, offered as

During the Cold War, several Eastern European countries began a process of rearmament with a majority of their industrial potential dedicated to the production and development of all types of weapons systems. The countries specialized in the manufacture of various elements: from personal weapons to transport and equipment trucks; Czechoslovakian companies manufactured these trucks.

TRACTOR TRUCK

A powerful MTU 12V engine powers this T 816 VWN9T tractor truck; it has 610 horsepower to tow cargo weighing fifty tons. It also has a large and comfortable cab, equipped with air conditioning.

TECHNICAL CHARACTERISTICS OF THE TATRA T 816 8 X 8.1R HEAVY TACTICAL TRUCK

COST IN DOLLARS:	Not available		Gas tank capacity	450 l
DIMENSIONS:			**PROPULSION:**	
Length	from 378 to 390 in depending on platform		DEUTZ BF 8M 1015C V8 turbodiesel engine and 544 hp	
Height	123.72 in until cab roof		**PERFORMANCE:**	
Width	98.5 in		Longitudinal gradient	75 %
Ground clearance	15.76 in		Depth of crossed body of water	49.25 in
WEIGHT:			Vertical obstacle	23.64 in
Empty	37,045 lbs		Maximum speed	68 mph
Maximum	143,325 lbs		Turn radius	88.65 feet
Maximum cargo	38,585 lbs		Range	435 miles

This Tatra 8x8 truck has been exported to an unidentified country in the Persian Gulf because of its excellent mobility and high transport capacity.

the T 815 21VV45 4 x 4.IR/30T, is a truck with two axles, which incorporates a T3B928 turbocharged V8 diesel with engine which produces 310 horsepower. It can transport a vehicle of 8.9 tons (and a cargo of 5.2 tons), reach a maximum speed of 75 mph and overcome obstacle with a 100 % gradient.

Even more capable is the 6 x 6 T815 21VV 26 variant with a chassis of three axles and six wheels that can transport cargo weighing up to 10 tons. However, it consumes 60 liters of fuel every 100 km. The T 815 WVN is similar to this last model but with a redesigned cab and a smaller cargo capacity. The T 815 VT with four axles is capable of carrying 10 tons of cargo and towing 25 tons over all types of terrain and 100 tons on the road. It is equipped with a double cab with space for half a dozen people, which is very useful for transporting weapons systems operators.

Specific offer to satisfy potential clients

The growth potential of the Czech industry is remarkable, and it is expected that, with Western aid, it can reach the level of its European counterparts in the next few years. This process entails that it first

EIGHT-WHEEL-DRIVE
The Tatra T 815 VT 26 is a heavy truck with a 265 hp engine; it has a cargo capacity of 10 tons in the rear and can tow up to 100 tons on the highway, which means it can recover vehicles of 110,250 lbs.

become a member of NATO and, probably, the European Union. This industrial capacity comes, on one hand, from the availability of qualified workers, who earn considerably lower wages than their Western counterparts, and on the other hand, from the maintenance of a high enough level of technological industrial capacity to deal with unsophisticated raw materials as in case of trucks, which are fitted out to a higher specification so as to obtain orders from abroad.

From the smallest trucks to the most powerful ones

The T 816 series is hoped to bring in a lot of export contracts. Several hundred of the 8 x 8 configuration have been ordered by a country in the Persian Gulf, probably the United Arab Emirates. The smallest in the range is a 4 x 4 with a 270 hp engine with some very important features. These include an empty weight of 9.2 tons, a capacity to carry cargo weighing up to 6 tons in the rear and tow up to 15 tons, and a reduced size (304.56 inches long and 98.5 inches wide). It also has a maximum speed of 56 mph and can traverse 100 % gradients, if its empty weight does not exceed 33,075 lbs, and 38 % gradients carrying the maximum amount of cargo.

Much more powerful and capable is the 8 x 8IR, configured with a large front cab and a cargo hold designed to transport different items such as: standard containers, hydraulic systems (to unload the cargo on the ground quickly and efficiently), fuel cisterns, and large tanks or containers with artillery projectiles. Its empty weight is 37,045 lbs, and it can carry up to 38,585 lbs. In addition, the radio has a range of close to 435 miles, and it has a Cargotec Multilift MK IV multi-platform with an articulated part in the cargo hold for loading and unloading the transported materials.

FRONT WHEEL ASSEMBLY
The special features of the wheel assembly of Tatra trucks is demonstrated is this photo, which shows how the front tires fall inward when they are not in contact with the ground.

VERY FLEXIBLE CHASSIS
This photo shows the flexibility of Tatra trucks, equipped with a wheel assembly capable of adapting to the irregularities of the terrain.

The T816 6VWN9T 43 tow truck has a similar configuration, although with a larger cab. It is designed to transport trailers that can carry combat tanks, artillery systems or all types of vehicles weighing under 43 tons.

Solutions tailor-made for each client

Many models have been developed based on various series of these Czech trucks due to the superior performance of the chassis, the remarkable appearance of the finished product (especially keeping in mind the asking price), their wide range of operational uses and their adaptation to transport requirements. Among the vehicles modeled after Tatra trucks is a 4 x 4 variant of the T 816, manufactured with a cab with armor-plating on its metallic components. It is also equipped with anti-bullet glass and a door on the top, which can be used to access a small stand for medium-weight machine guns. There are other 4 x 4 models, configured as mobile maneuvers workshops, launchers of JOJKA automatic-pilot reconnaissance vehicles, or POP-2 hospitals for the injured with an operating room on the flat bed.

Some models based on 6 x 6 trucks are AVS cranes to recover other vehicles, CAP-6 cisterns with their own pump system, the ACHR-90 for decontaminating biological, chemical or nuclear agents, the TAMARA for transporting equipment to pick up radar signals, and the TATRAPAN with full armor-plating on the cab and cargo hold. 8 x 8 trucks are used to configure models like the PMS for transporting a floating bridge element, the AM-50B with a collapsible bridge, the VZ-92 for transporting an automatic mine sapper, or the VZ-70 with a 122 millimeter multiple rocket launcher, ZUZANA 155 mm mortar (mobile and very powerful) or the STROP anti-air artillery system.

THE SMALLEST OF THE RANGE

The Czech firm Tatra produces a wide range of trucks; the T 815 series is part of its smaller models.

LOGISTICAL TRANSPORT

The Tatra range includes 4x4 trucks designed for the logistical transport of men and various materials, such as this unit from the T 815 series with a 5 ton cargo capacity.

The need that military troops and some civilian bodies have to move over all types of terrain has led to the development of various vehicles designed to travel over mountain roads, rocky ground, snow-covered areas and even lakes and flowing rivers.

The most well known and capable models have emerged in those countries that need to incorporate them into their Armed Forces because of difficult climates. Such is the case with the Nordic countries, although their vehicles have also had a lot of success in all corners of the world, from the Cambodian jungle to the Alaskan tundra, because of their superior performance and ample operational uses.

Need intensifies the productive device

In order to replace the Volvo Bv 202, widely distributed amongst the Swedish Army during the 1960's and beginning of the 1970's, the Swedish Administration of Defense Materials decided to test out new proposals. In 1974, they gave the contract for development to Hägglund and Söner, which developed various batches of prototypes from 1976-1978.

TRANSFORMED FOR COMBAT

The Bv 206S is a version of the Swedish Bv 206 with a modified back cab and armor plating on all its bodywork so that it can withstand the impact of lightweight weapons and the effects of grenade explosions in its vicinity.

Good performance leads to a quick approval

Its capacity to travel over all types of terrain led to the purchase of the first units of a model called Bv 206; the pre-production batch was delivered in 1980. The first Swedish order, a country that currently has more than four thousand of these double-cab vehicles, was followed by an order from Norway in 1981 for 220 units and in 1985 for 2,004 more.

Recently, orders have been filled for a total of more than 10,000 units. Great Britain

ordered 600 for its Army, Air Force and Royal Marines; the United States uses 1,100 of the M973 SUSV (Small Unit Support Vehicle); the Spanish Army purchased thirty mainly for use in the "Aragón" 1 Mountain Hunter Brigade; France has incorporated them into their 27th Mountain Division; Canada uses 100, and there are also units used in Germany, Brazil, Chile, China, Holland, Italy, Pakistan and Singapore. Singapore ordered 300 units in 1993, and it is possible, with the development of new models like the Bv 206S armor-plated variant with total protection for all personnel and the new Bv 209, that they will order more. The Bv 209 is an updated model of the 206S with a more advanced engine, more comfortable interior and better protection against various enemy threats.

Superior features and proven efficiency

The Bv 206 basically consists of 2 small waterproof cabs powered by rubber tracks; the first cab is a tractor and tows the second. Manufactured from very resistant, reinforced

FAMILY OF VARIOUS MODELS

The NA series of off-road vehicles includes several configurations of the rear cab transformed into a mobile crane, a logistical shelter, a communications vehicle, a weapons transporter, a command post or an evacuation ambulance.

lightweight plastic fiber, the first cab holds the driver and four more men, while the second, with two benches, can carry up to eleven men or various weapons systems. Many versions have been configured from this basic design, such as anti-tank models with the RBS 56 Bill system, RBS 90 air defense models with vehicles to transport the radar and

VERY RECENT VARIANT

The Bv 209 is a transformation of the Swedish Bv 206, which incorporates several improvements and complete armor-plating for a greater capacity for movement in the combat zone.

others, RBS 70, to transport the missile firing squads. There are also variants for anti-air detection with radar detection devices such as the Ericsson Giraffe 50 AT in the C frequency band and models with 81 or 120 millimeter mortar. Finally, there are medical evacuation variants, which are used by the British and Dutch Marines, maintenance vehicles with a crane and a hydraulic towline, rescue vehicles and fire trucks used in the Maldives and by the British Royal Air Force, and command post models with radar equipment in the interior.

Powered by a Mercedes Benz diesel engine with 136 horsepower at 4,600 r.p.m., although some units use gasoline engines, these vehicles can reach a maximum speed of 32 mph on the road and 1.86 mph in flowing rivers. They have an empty weight of 9,900 pounds, and a maximum cargo of 1,345 lbs in the front cab and 3,615 in the rear one. They can also tow flat beds or cargo weighing up to 2.5 tons with the hook on the second cab.

Other important feature of this Swedish vehicle is the width of its tracks, 225 inches, which are lightweight enough so that it may drive over snow or on the shore of lakes or oceans, where the sand is fine. Its weight also reduces the risk of detonating any half-buried anti-tank mines that it comes across.

The large market leads to the appearance of new models

Favorable sales prospects have led various companies to design specific products; some of these have been created from the militari-

> **OPERATIONAL POSSIBILITIES**
> The ease with which they move over the most difficult terrain, their capacity to transport 15 men and 2 tons of material, and the potential to configure them as evacuation ambulances or mobile command posts are some of the features which define Bv 206 vehicles.

> **UNRESTRICTED MOVEMENT**
> Designed to operate over difficult and mountainous terrain, where snow, flowing rivers and rugged ground are common, the Bv 206 can easily traverse 100 % gradients as long as the surface is solid.

zation of civilian vehicles used on ski slopes. One of these is the Kässbohrer Flexmobil FM 23, which has been used by UN personnel deployed in Lebanon. It consists of a front caterpillar track unit with room for up to 10 people and a rear flat bed for towing cargo weighing up to 2,650 lbs. It is German and has excellent performance capabilities due to the two wide caterpillar tracks that optimize its stability.

A Finnish alternative arrives on the scene

Produced by the Finnish company, Patria Vehicles, the Sisu NA-140 is very similar to the Swedish Bv 206 model. It was tested in 1985, and the next year 11 pre-production units were ordered. Since then, more than three hundred have been manufactured to equip the armies of China, Turkey and Finland. This last country has purchased units of the most advanced variants such as the NA-122, which incorporates a 120 mm mortar in the cargo hold with three system operators and 18 highly explosive projectiles.

The NA-140 is multi-purpose and very adaptable to all kinds of necessities. It has a very compact size and is very agile due to its 6.5 liter diesel engine with 129 hp and a

weight is 17,300 lbs. It is expected that the general cargo variant, called the P6-300M, will be manufactured in addition to other models for transporting equipment cabs, weapons launchers or logistical elements.

maximum speed of 37 mph. It has a cargo capacity of five men in the front cab and 12 in the rear, ample operational possibilities as it is amphibious and may be transported by air, and a total cargo capacity of 2 tons (1.3 tons in the back cab).

Norway decides to test its own product

After almost twenty years of using the Bv 206, the Norwegian Armed Forces may incorporate up to 1,000 units of the Natech (Narvik Technology AS) P6 if Project 5085 is instituted. The project has already been approved by the Cabinet, and some prototypes have been tested since 1997 at the Army Material Command Testing and Trial Unit in Helgelandsmoen.

The vehicle is newly configured: it incorporates robust anti-capsizing bars on the front cab, which has room for five men; a very powerful Cummins 6CTA8 diesel engine with 260 hp, which can transport almost 7 tons, divided into 4.6 tons in the rear cab and 2.35 tons in the front; and a hydrostatics transmission, designed for greater possibility of movement over all types of terrain, especially snow-covered ground. It is 315 inches long, 94.56 wide and 102.44 high, and its empty

RAPID DEPLOYMENT

The large number of doors on the sides and rear of Bv 206 caterpillar tracks allow for the rapid evacuation of personnel in the case of enemy fire (bottom photograph).

DRIVER'S SEAT

The driver's seat is located on the front left side. This vehicle has a large steering wheel and some pedals, and it is maneuvered in much the same way as an automobile.

ACCESS DOORS

The front cab has two doors on each side so that half a dozen men can enter and leave the vehicle quickly.

INTEGRATED LIGHTS

The elements that allow for driving at night are located at the front of the main cab on the sides; these include powerful headlights, orange pilot lights for signaling movements and the war lights.

WHEEL ASSEMBLY

The mobility of this vehicle is based on two chains made of rubber and metal and a wheel assembly with a wheel motor, tractor wheels and four large metal support wheels, which enable the vehicle to move over land or in water.

OBSERVATION WINDOWS

Two large windows on each side of the cargo cab allow the personnel inside to observe what is happening outside and act accordingly.

TRANSPORT ZONE

A metal support on the upper part of the rear cab is used for carrying backpacks, munitions boxes or logistical packaging —anything the crew traveling inside might need.

REAR CAB

The rear caterpillar track module is waterproof and has two benches on the sides that can fit a dozen men with their backpacks and individual weapons, or up to 3,615 lbs of cargo.

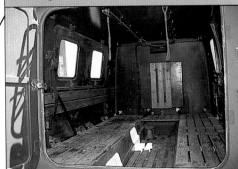

PROTECTED FROM DUST

The configuration and large size of the caterpillar tracks on the Bv 206 means that they stir up a considerable quantity of dust and dirt when driving over arid ground; therefore, the tow hook is located between two large rubber shirts on the bodywork at the back of the cab.

TECHNICAL CHARACTERISTICS OF THE BV 206 CATERPILLAR TRACK

COST IN DOLLARS:	132,000,000
DIMENSIONES:	
Length	271.86 in
Height	94.56 in
Width	78.8 in
Ground clearance	13.79
WEIGHT:	
Empty	6,040 lbs the front unit, and 3,815 lbs the back one
Maximum cargo	1,345 lbs the front unit, and 3,615 lbs the back one
Cargo in tow	5,515 lbs
PROPULSION:	
2,996 l Mercedes Benz OM 603.950.2 diesel engine with 6 cylinders and 136 hp at 4,600 r.p.m.	

PERFORMANCE:	
Longitudinal gradient	100 % on firm ground and 30 % on snow
Transversal gradient	30 %
Depth of crossed body of water	It is amphibious without any extra equipment
Maximum speed	32 mph on the road and 1.86 mph in water
Turn radius	The front unit can turn around itself in 20 feet
Range	185 miles

TABLE OF CONTENTS